SCALE MODEL
TUGS

SCALE MODEL TUGS

Tom Gorman

Special Interest Model Books

Special Interest Model Books Ltd
P.O.Box 327
Poole, Dorset BH15 2RG
England

First published 2009
Text © 2009 Tom Gorman
Layout © 2009 Special Interest Model Books Ltd
Design © Crispin Goodall Design

ISBN 978 185486 255 6

www.specialinterestmodelbooks.co.uk

Printed and bound in Great Britain by Martins the Printers
Berwick upon Tweed

Contents

Introduction

The data and information within this book comes mostly from my own experiences: initially from my early years spent on Tyneside and latterly during the building of a number of ship models and tugs, the full size vessels having been built on Humberside where I was fortunate to follow the actual building at the shipyard. A great deal of information comes also from the many friends and associates with whom I have worked over the years. This personal practical experience is allied to information gleaned from books such as British Steam Tugs by P. N. Thomas (Waine Research Publications) – which must surely be the model tug master's manual – and from similar sources of reference.

This book is written in order to provide information and data for those who wish to build and sail model tugs. There is a growing interest in tugs and many model boat clubs today run events, such as tug towing competitions, especially for the model tug owner. A national tug towing competition is run in the U.K. under the sponsorship of Mobile Marine Models, a company that specialises in making model tug kits and associated parts. Unfortunately, as U.K. shipyards close and such work is carried out abroad, the availability of information and drawings, etc.

relative to ships and tugs is sadly decreasing.

From many years of experience and with the invaluable assistance of a number of expert friends and fellow modellers, the following chapters will guide the model builder through the realms of the tug, both ancient and modern. To those who have helped and assisted me, too many to be named, I express my sincere thanks, their friendship is greatly appreciated.

The book is divided into 15 chapters, each designed to give information upon a certain aspect of modelling and thus to provide the modeller with a source of reference.

Today, there is a much wider range of kits available to assist the prospective modeller in building a fine range of scale model ships, and within such kits there are a number that also include the subject of this book. Details of these kits are given in the following chapters – and in order to give the newcomer to the hobby, full photographic and written descriptions are included that relate to the building of the specific model tugs featured in the kit. All of the photographs

Tug 'AK BURKUT' loading from stern at quayside.

are by the author unless otherwise stated – and it should be noted that some of the photographs that accompany Chapter 11 are not of tug models, but are included in order to illustrate steam outfits.

Some detail is also provided on producing a model tug from basic materials (i.e. building from scratch) and theses chapters cover the many, separate parts of construction and completing a model – whether it be a fully-working and radio-controlled unit or one designed for display only.

The initial chapters provide introductory information leading to more detailed data in later chapters. Development of the tug as a specific type of vessel is covered, from the earliest steam-driven craft to the latest and most sophisticated vessels.

Other chapters deal with model motive power, whether steam or electric, and whilst it is not possible to give finite data on the sizing of some drive equipment within the limits of a book of this type, good and sensible guidance is given wherever possible. Further chapters provide information on radio equipment, selection and installation, and space is given to details of deck machinery and equipment that is visible on the tug. There is also advice on painting and finishing the model and how and where the necessary navigation lights are installed (and on how they can be illuminated if required).

Finally, there is also information on preparing the model for display or for competition, along with some details of model boat clubs and the competitions available. Among these, tug-towing competitions are popular, as are steering contests, where model ships are sailed through a set course to gain points for accuracy. Some regattas also have sections where models are judged for their accuracy and quality off the sailing water.

Top: Tug 'AK BURKUT' loading cable to own towing winch

Centre: Model of tug AYTON CROSS test sailing at Oates water

Bottom: AYTON CROSS showing some detailing.

Chapter 1

Tugs in General

The tug, as a specific ship type, first appeared in the early part of the nineteenth following the development of the steam engine. Initially, they were designed specifically to pull large sailing vessels from port to the open sea and vice versa. Tugs often also aided fishing vessels by collecting their catches and delivering them to port more quickly than was possible under sail. The manoeuvring of large ships in harbours and docks was also a very large part of the tug use in those early days because gaining steerage way is difficult for a large ship in confined waters. Regrettably, the advent and design of bow and stern thrusters and other steering aids for many types of large vessels has removed the need for the tug. Nevertheless, tugs are still in demand in order to handle the large container ships and oil tankers that are driven by a single screw – and where long lengths and deep draughts negate the use of athwartships thrusters. Overall, though, it is obvious that the ship which can berth without the need for tugs will save money – and commercial shipping is all about money.

Tugs can be divided roughly into four categories as follows:

Harbour Tugs – General-purpose, small ships designed to operate within the confines of the harbour or river in which they worked. Often little more than a large engine surrounded by a ship's shell, they were of as deep a draft as could be accommodated in the operating waters, a deep draft at the stern being essential to allow the propeller(s) to exert maximum thrust. The tow hook was usually attached to a suitably strengthened part of the after superstructure. Accommodation was very basic, allowing only for daily use and so without sleeping berths or cabins. Each tug usually carried a small boat, and the engine room skylights and other parts of the after decks were protected by towing bows to guide the ropes freely.

Paddle tug ZEELAND. *Photo courtesy of Deans Marine.*

FURIE vintage tug. *Photo courtesy of Deans Marine.*

River Tugs – Not quite as restricted as the harbour tugs; but in many rivers they also had to enter the confines of docks, where restrictions required that they too had to be designed to suit the areas in which they worked. Frequently, such tugs would be required to handle barges, both laden and unladen, and also to tow hoppers of spoil dredged from the river channels out to dumping grounds offshore. Thus, they were built beamier and with more sheer in order to withstand the weather and rigours of the open sea. The outfit of these tugs included the same equipment as the harbour tug, often supplemented by radar and fire monitors so that they could assist in handling shipboard fires.

Coastal Tugs – Generally larger and suitable for coastal towing when there was insufficient work in the river or harbour from where they generally worked. Accommodation included cabin berths for the crew and officers, as the vessels often worked continuously for periods of some days. Their powerful engines gave them a reasonable turn of speed so that they could answer distress calls. In fact, 15 to 18 knots was not unusual. As with the smaller tugs, they had tow hooks attached to the after part of the superstructure and they frequently had two sizes of hook to cater for differing tows. The modern coastal tug generally has a large towing winch used in preference to the hook so that the length of the tow could be varied according to where they were operating. Two lifeboats in davits were usual and often a small workboat would be carried beneath the tow bows on the stern deck. Radio, radar and

sounding equipment was usually as sophisticated as cost would allow. The modern coastal tug today generally carries a rigid inflatable boat and life raft canisters in place of lifeboats. The instruments nowadays include satellite navigation and ship to shore mobile phones and computers.

Ocean-going Tugs – Much larger than the above types and designed for both long ocean voyages and for salvage work, as well as having a fairly high running speed in order to allow them to attend to a ship in distress as quickly as possible. They usually carry a range of equipment such as compressors, pumps and generators, etc. so as to service a ship suffering engine room failure, flooding or other damage. The accommodation is generous and will most likely have air-conditioning and enclosed superstructures to allow crews to work comfortably in all weathers and areas, varying from tropical waters to the Arctic. They carry large lifeboats and use an automatic towing winch system in preference to hooks for towing. One or more heavy lift derricks or cranes are generally fitted in order to handle the equipment; and the towing beams over the after deck are high enough to allow crew members to walk beneath them.

There are and were other tug types that do not fall into the above categories such as the Thames lighterage tugs sized and built and used almost exclusively for moving barges through the bridges over the river. There is also the tug tender built not

GRIBBIN HEAD Harbour tug. *Photo courtesy of Mobile Marine Models.*

only for towing but also for carrying passenger and luggage from shore to large liners or cruise ships at anchor offshore or in the deep waters of an estuary. These tugs make excellent models but at the time of writing there are no kits produced of the tug tender pattern vessel. The intending modeller will have to work from drawings and build the hull in the plank-on-frame or bread-and-butter fashion as described later in chapter nine.

In the early days, tugs were driven by paddles and relatively crude steam engines and boilers. Development of the steam engine and boiler, together with the feathering paddle, soon brought the paddle tug into extensive use. In fact, paddle-driven tugs were in use by the Admiralty into the 1960s. Drawings of many paddle-driven tugs can be found in the libraries of many plans services (see Appendix 2).

Some companies produce hulls for model paddle tugs – and at the time of writing, one paddle tug, Glasgow, is available in kit form from the German kit-makers Graupner. This kit includes beautifully-made, fully-feathering paddles to a scale of 1:30. The paddle sets are made in hard plastic and are available as separate kits for those who wish to build a different paddle tug.

Paddle tugs had independent paddle control and were capable of turning within their own length. However, in model form, it is much wiser to link the paddles together and drive them from a single source. There is a good reason for this: running one paddle full ahead and the other full astern can very quickly cause the model to capsize. There is also the additional problem that when independent driving motors are used, it is hard to find a pair to run at identical speeds. Thus, unless rudder is applied, the model tends to turn continuously to one side or the other as well as it having a tendency to waddle like a duck over the water! Details of feathering paddles are shown in Figs 1/2 & 1/3. They require care in construction but are definitely not beyond the capabilities of the average modeller.

Kits for building screw-driven tugs are available from a number of manufacturers both in the U.K. and overseas. One manufacturer, Mobile Marine Models (see Appendix 2) specialises in model tugs to a standard scale of 1:32 and has a quite extensive range available. In fact, most kit makers in the U.K. have one or more tugs in their range.

AFON BRAINT tug under construction at Paull, Humberside

Right Fig 1.01: Fixed float pattern paddle wheel.

Below right Fig 1.02: Feathering paddle wheel with outer ring.

Of course, as with all commercially produced equipment, there is a wide variance of what is included as an integral part of the kit and it is incumbent upon the modeller to ensure that he/she realises any shortcomings and makes provision for any additional parts that may be needed. In general, when purchased, a full kit will contain all the materials and parts – except for adhesives and paint – that are required to build the model. However, rarely will the kit contain drive equipment or radio control gear. Consequently, the cost of such equipment will need to be added to the cost of the kit. Some makers offer a semi-kit service where the whole outfit is inclusive of adhesives and drive gear, but excluding radio controls. Paint can be purchased in separate quantities at separate times, thereby spreading costs over the build period, e.g. purchasing, in order, the hull in GRP (or g.r.p, being glass reinforced plastic) and drawings; then timber for decks, superstructure, etc. with templates; followed by drive equipment and then fittings as required.

The novice or newcomer to model tug building will be wise to buy a simple kit to start with. From this, they will gain experience in building and most kit makers have such small and simpler kits within their range. In addition, almost all kit makers are usually happy to offer advice and assistance to the modeller. Nevertheless, but it is probably sensible for any new modeller to join the local or nearest model boat club. There, members are usually very helpful and there will be a lake or pond on which the model, once completed, can be sailed. Incidentally, it should not be assumed that model ship building is the domain of the male, and there are many very fine female ship modellers whose work is of very high quality indeed.

Over the last few decades, there have been developments in the propulsion systems of the modern tug. Today, many are fitted at the very least with twin screws and with bow thrusters. Further, almost all screw-driven tugs have Kort nozzles surrounding the propeller(s) and many of the Kort nozzles have rudders attached and are thereby steerable. The development of other propulsion units has been an ongoing process and many modern tugs are now fitted with azimuthing propeller systems at bow and stern – enabling such tugs to operate as easily astern as ahead. More frequently, modern tugs – particularly ship-handling tugs – are being fitted with Voith Schneider propeller systems that allow rapid movement changes in all directions. Developments in compression ignition (diesel) engines have allowed increases in propulsive power with savings in size and weight of the engine along with fuel economy. The newer drive system developments have also allowed control of the ship to be made from the bridge, thus negating the use of an engine room telegraph and giving the tug master immediate response to a movement of rudder or engine. All these developments have made the tug a better and more efficient unit, with services geared to alternative work rather than just the simple task of towing that was required in earlier days.

Throughout the ensuing chapters, you will find

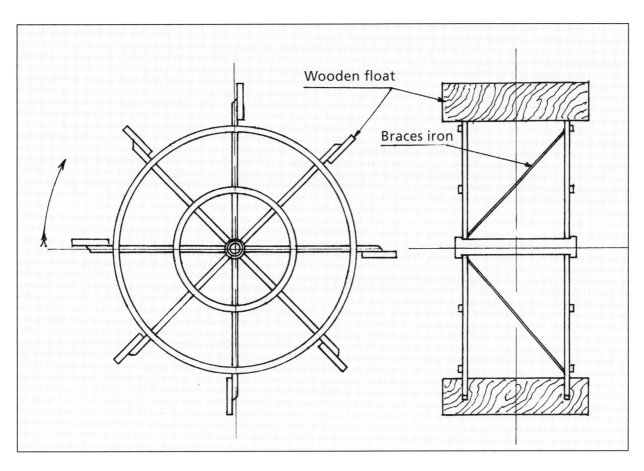

Wooden float

Braces iron

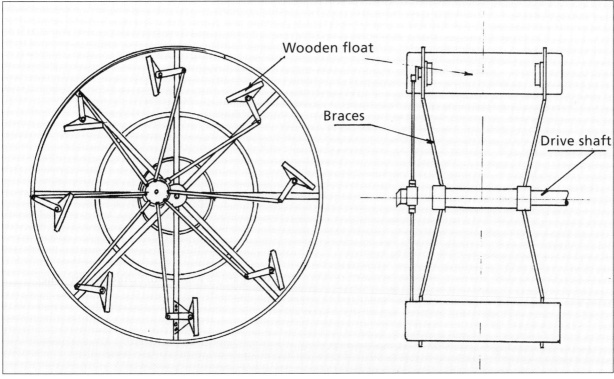

Wooden float

Braces

Drive shaft

it unnecessary to have a supply of sophisticated and expensive tools, as it is perfectly possible to build a fine, static or working model with just a few good quality tools. However, it is wise to buy the very best tools that you can afford; cheap tools rarely do the job for which they are intended and the often fail very quickly. It is also worth noting that it is not the sharp,

keen tool that slips and cuts the user, but the blunt one that needs extra (and often too much) force to effect the cut.

Building from a kit requires fewer tools than building with raw materials from scratch. The following will probably be sufficient to start the work: a good, sharp craft knife (preferably of the snap-off blade type);

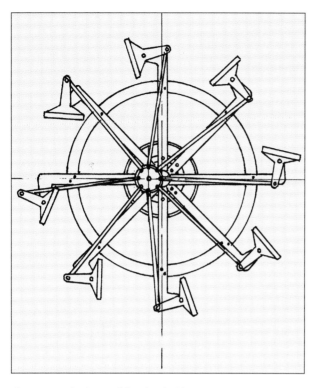

Fig 1.03: Feathering paddle wheel without outer ring

Model of tug ENGLISHMAN in commercial service – *photo courtesy of Model Slipway.*

• a steel rule;
• a cutting mat to avoid losing blade points;
• a small drill with a selection of bits;
• a selection of small files;
• a glasspaper block.

Those kits containing timber and plywood parts will show the need for a small handsaw or fretsaw – but fine plywood can be successfully cut with a sharp craft knife and a steel rule. A stainless steel twelve-inch rule is ideal for modelling work, but for preference, should be marked with both imperial and metric measurements.

Many modern ship kits make extensive use of styrene (plastic) sheet (or 'plasticard' as it is sometimes called) and the sheets are often printed with the outlines and details of the section of kit referred to. This material is clean and easy to use – it is simply cut by scoring along the cutting line after which it can be snapped apart. The scoring raises a bead along the edges of the sheet that needs to be removed – by sanding or scraping along the edge with the edge of the knife blade – before being joined to neighbouring parts. In fact, there is a relatively inexpensive small tool, sold by craft shops and artists supply stores, that is specifically designed for cutting plastic sheet without producing a raised edge. (Possible stockist include Squires – see Appendix 2 for other tool stockists).

Joining plastic (styrene) parts together is best done using liquid polystyrene cement and a small fine brush. The parts to be joined should be held together

Full size Damen tug on water 'Smit Hmber'.

Stern deck detail of Damen tug.

lightly, the brush charged with adhesive should be drawn along the joint and the joint held for a few seconds. The liquid welds the two parts together by chemical action and the pieces can be handled after a few minutes, However, the joint will not be fully cured for at least 12 hours and sanding or cleaning for painting should not be done too soon after the joints are effected.

Adhesives for joining timber to timber abound; but for a joint that will withstand immersion in water the best is Cascamite, which comes in powder form and has to be mixed with clean water to form a thick cream before use. It is resin glue that has a very slow cure time so that parts joined with Cascamite will need to be held or clamped together for some hours in order to allow the joint to become firm. A 'quicker-grabbing' adhesive for timber – but not quite so impervious to water – is PVA (polyvinyl acetate), a glue of the aliphatic type. This is also a resin glue, of creamy white appearance, that dries hard to a transparent finish and has a grab time of only a few minutes. Parts can actually be hand-held until the PVA glue sets. Again, though, the full cure

of the adhesive is not reached for some 12 hours after use. Thus, in the same way as with liquid polystyrene cement, the joints need to be left for some hours before they are sanded and prepared for painting or other work.

For joining dissimilar materials, such as styrene sheet to timber, surfaces should first be roughened in order to provide a key for the adhesive. Cyanoacrylate (so-called 'Superglue') is probably best, although one of the several types of two-part epoxy cements may suffice. For metal-to-timber or metal-to-styrene adhesion, then superglue is probably the best choice. When joining timber or styrene to GRP (g.r.p. or

15

glass reinforced plastic), the best adhesive is catalysed polyester resin, but two-part epoxy resin of the slow-cure type will also suffice. Details of these and other adhesives are given throughout the ensuing chapters.

As explained earlier, there are several different types of tugs and so it is not possible to describe the building of each and every one. However, the similarities of one with another will become apparent with continued experience and the descriptions of building a model within this book are of a general pattern that ought to be applicable to most models.

The details and photographs included are selected to show the section of work described and in many cases are of different models. Wherever possible, captions accompanying the photographs will refer to places within the text, where there is more information. The reader will find too that there are photographs and descriptions of full-size tugs, some shown under construction and some in working order. Where possible too, photographs of tow hooks, towing winches, windlasses and deck machinery are included to provide details of such machinery and to aid accurate reproduction in miniature.

In the following chapters, the methods and sequences of building model tugs are those favoured by the writer and found by him to give the best results – but they are not hidebound and are offered only in order to give the modeller as much practical help as possible. They are based upon the experiences gained in many years of building models, not only tugs but of other types of ships, for a number of clients.

Each type of tug is described as accurately as possible so as to assist the modeller to select the one that best meets with his/her requirements. Obviously, though, each modeller will have look at his/her models drawings and instructions and make decisions on how to complete each section of the construction. Yet, a little advice is always helpful. For example, there will be a number of small parts and/or small kits that can be completed at almost any time during the currency of the work. The modeller can build these while waiting for glue to cure or paint to dry on other models; and it is always advisable to paint some parts before they are installed on the model. Also, very small parts – such as bollards and fairleads – can, after cleaning, be mounted on a piece of scrap timber using double-sided adhesive tape. In this way, they can be held securely for painting, by either brush or spray. Equally obvious is the fact that the sensible modeller will, having purchased the selected kit, read the instructions and examine all the parts provided – thereby enabling decisions regarding painting, assembly, etc. to be made early in the building programme and reducing errors to a minimum. After all, regardless of experience, we all make mistakes; the expert merely reduces his/hers to a bare minimum by good planning.

Habour Tugs

As described in the previous chapter, tugs fall into fairly clear categories; that is, they did until comparatively recent times – but more of that later. Tugs of the small harbour and river workboat pattern make attractive, small models and they can be built to a larger scale than is the case when modelling bigger vessel. This helps when making details, because such details and small parts of models – built to a small scale – are much harder to make than those built to a large scale.

Harbour tugs can still be found in service today, with some having only been built very recently. In general, such tugs are less complex than the larger vessels and they are, therefore, a more suitable type to attempt for the modeller with little experience.

As an indication of how the harbour tug design has changed over the years, illustrations can be found in a number of books that feature paddle tugs for harbour and river use. Some of these early tugs and paddle tugs have survived in preservation; and some actually carried on operating into the mid-1970s. As mentioned in the previous chapter, there is just one kit of a paddle tug available today: that of the *Glasgow* and produced by Graupner in Germany (see Appendix 2). This is a harbour tug and can be fitted with a small steam plant – although the models are usually electrically driven. This kit is within the capability of the newcomer to model shipbuilding, but it is not recommended for the complete novice, i.e. one without any previous model-building experience. Any such novice builder would be better advised to select a single-screw, simpler model type such as *Neptune* or others that are illustrated in this book.

Of course, the steam engine was the prime source of power in all early tugs. In order to replicate

WYEFORCE small tug. *Photo courtesy Model Slipway.*

AFON BRAINT completed and being fitted out in Hull docks

Right above: T I D type tug LEA model under way

Right below: ANGLIAN MAN model. *Photo courtesy Mobile Marine Models*

this, small steam engines and boiler plants are still available today from specialist suppliers and the larger model stores. Thus, a small harbour tug built from a kit can be outfitted with a small steam unit specially made for miniature use, e.g. the Minivap range.

By present day standards, these steam outfits are not too expensive and compare reasonably in cost with the more sophisticated electric drive equipment. It is necessary, however, to buy the steam plant from a reputable maker and to ensure that it carries a full set of test certificates – as such certificates are required to be shown to the officials of model clubs when visiting their lakes or ponds before permission is given for the model to be sailed upon the water under the club's control (see Chapters 14 and 15 for more details). All things considered, it is probably better for the novice and/or newcomer to model ship building to fit a simple electric drive for a first model, Suitable types of electric and steam drives are described in later chapters.

With the development of the diesel engine and suitable gearboxes, tugs converted to this method of propulsion very quickly – particularly as a diesel engine can be started and be in service within a few minutes, whereas the steam plant needs several hours to reach its operating state if the boiler has been allowed to go cold. The gearbox is, of course, an essential part of a small marine diesel engine, as it cannot be reversed as can a steam engine. It is also through the gearbox that the high revolutions of the compression ignition engine are reduced to suit the propeller system. Indeed, as far as I can ascertain,

there are no tugs in service that utilise a direct drive system. Large ships, such as tankers and container vessels, use very large and slow-running compression ignition engines where only straightforward reversal is needed and can sometimes be carried out by the engine.

Modern harbour tugs such as *Wyeforce* are twin-screw driven, having twin diesel engines and gearboxes. This allows for easy manoeuvring in confined areas and gives the tug the ability to work easily when in close proximity to its main ship.

Some of the photographs in the book show the tug *Afon Alaw* when under construction at the builder's yard of Hepworth's at Paull on Humberside. These photographs show the twin screws in Kort nozzles of the fixed pattern quite clearly along with other aspects of the tug when on the building slip. Other photographs show a model tug from the Mobile Marine Models range under construction by the author.

The model *Wyeforce* comes from the Model Slipway range of ship kits. It can be completed fairly quickly and when fitted with good quality drive motors, can provide a good bollard pull. Bollard pull is the

yardstick by which tugs are compared. Each tug, when new and on trials, is required to haul against a static bollard with equipment that can measure, in tons, how strongly the tug pulls. This information is then available to all who need it. One model of *Wyeforce* known to the writer was found capable of a pull of some 2 kilograms (4½ lb) as measured with a spring balance and with the model running full ahead.

Many of the modern harbour tugs utilise differing drive systems, some using azimuth thrusters and some Voith Schneider drive units. Both of these patterns of drive unit are available in model form, but (at the time of writing) only in one scale. They are both produced by the German company Graupner,

SMIT FRANKRIJK. *Photo courtesy of Deans Marine.*

whose products are distributed in the U.K. and are available from most good model shops (see Appendix 2). Technically, although the units produced by Graupner are similar to azimuthing units, they are in fact Schottel drive units and can only turn through 240 degrees – whereas an azimuthing unit can revolve through the full 360 degrees. Both these units seem to be scaled at 1:50, which naturally restricts their use to models built to this scale. As far as can be ascertained, these units are unlikely to be made to alternative scales in the foreseeable future.

The propulsion equipment (running gear) of most kit model tugs is confined to conventional shafts and propellers. Nevertheless, there is a very wide range of model propellers produced for the model ship builder. They are available direct from makers or through the larger model shops and those smaller outlets that specialise in marine modelling equipment. (Chapters 10 and 11 deal more fully with propulsion equipment.)

The use of the Kort nozzle is widespread in the tug world. Such nozzles are available from a number of sources, but the prospective user should be aware that the propellers needed for use with a Kort nozzle have to be made to suit the nozzle with blades that follow the curve of the nozzle and cannot be of the conventionally shaped kind. Some vessels are fitted with fixed Kort nozzles that have the rudder(s) in line astern, while others have nozzles that are arranged to turn and have the rudder blade attached to the nozzle. Amongst modellers, there is some debate as to which of these is the better arrangement. The nozzle turning about the fixed rudder produces a greater space between the blade tip, whilst the Kort ring suggests a small loss in efficiency. Many expert opinions are that this loss is negated by better and quicker turning. As a modeller, you pay your money and make your choice – but my personal preference is for the fixed nozzle, it being easier to install and control.

Chapter 3

Coastal Tugs

Coastal tugs, such as those used for moving large vessels quite long distances between ports or up the bigger river estuaries – for example the Humber, Bristol Channel, etc. – are different, in many ways, from their smaller, harbour sisters. Usually, such tugs have some degree of accommodation, which allows for the crew to live in board for a short period during extended towing duties.

Obviously, coastal tugs are, larger vessels than the harbour tug and are fitted with more powerful engines and frequently carry two tow hooks of different sizes to accommodate the range of vessels they have to handle. Generally speaking, they have high bows and a deep sheer that permit them to work reasonably safely in heavy weather and high seas.

In the tug's early days, the accommodation was Spartan indeed, the whole idea of the tug being that of a workhorse with little thought being given to the comfort of the crew. After all, a tug was little more than a vehicle for a large and powerful engine with its accompanying boiler plant, This configuration prevailed from the early days right up to shortly after World War II, when many aspects of Merchant Navy life were changed by legislation.

The modern coastal tug is much better geared to the comfort of the crew, with more thought given to the working conditions of the personnel. The tug master has a great responsibility towards the tow and its value. He needs to be fully aware of the effect of wind, tide and current upon his tow, particularly if it is not under some degree of power. His expertise must include knowledge of the estuaries, rivers and coasts which he trades and, above all, he must know the capabilities of his tug to the last possible degree. Today, with fewer in service, the range of duties for the coastal tug have been seriously depleted and there is a tendency for the modern tug to be designed not only for harbour duty but also for coastal service.

In the days of the steam screw and paddle tugs, the distinction between the various types of tug was quite marked. Yet, today, there is often very little to choose between them other than size. This is reflected in the kits that are available to build models of some of these types of tug. As the illustrations show, some of these kits cover a range of single-screw tugs and some

AL KHUBAR 2 *Photo courtesy Model Slipway*

twin-screw units. Model tug kits are also available within the ranges from continental European makers, the biggest range coming from Billings (see Appendix 2), who have a number of tugs of varying sizes in their catalogue.

In fact, the very first model ship that the author constructed was a tug called Zwarte Zee from a Billings kit that is still available. This kit included all the necessary timber to build the hull plank-on-frame and it taught the author a great deal about building hulls from line drawings. It was an exercise more like building from scratch than from a kit, although the inclusion of a detailed instruction manual did help. Currently, the widest range of tug kits is produced by Mobile Marine Models in the U.K. (see Appendix 2).

Many modern harbour tugs are fitted with towing winches in addition to a tow hook. Such winches allow the tug to reduce or lengthen the distance of the tow to effect better control during towing. They are generally large, fitted immediately aft of the superstructure and often partly covered by the boat deck above in order to give a degree of shelter to the operators. In some cases there will be a second winch fitted near the bow, often forming part of the windlass, to permit the tug to tow when running astern. In both cases, there will be quite substantial

load guides (fairleads) to ensure the tow rope is fed to the winch correctly.

It should also be noted that many modern tugs have their navigation lights at port and starboard sides duplicated inversely – so as to permit the ship to show the correct running colour according to the direction in which it is running. Details are given in Chapter 14 along with diagrams in Appendix 5 of the patterns of navigation lights that can be expected.

The many harbour tug kits available include a variety of types. For example, some comprise a box containing a supply of strip wood (for planking the hull), a set of drawings, an instruction booklet, a set of pre-cut parts (to form keel, hull frames, deck superstructure, etc.) and a supply of fittings, often in white metal and sometimes with some in resin. In general, there will also be a propeller shaft (or shafts) and wire and rod from which to make guard rails, etc. A kit like this is as near as one can get to building a model from scratch, even though the materials are pre-selected.

The next step up the line is called semi-kit. This generally contains a pre-made hull, a good scale drawing, some templates (from which to make various sections of the model), materials from which to make decks, superstructures, etc. and a selection

Top: AZIZ tug and support vessel. *Photo courtesy Model Slipway*

Above left: Cory tug ROWANGARTH on river Tees. *Photo courtesy of Mobile Marine*

Above: Tug NEWCASTLE *Photo courtesy of Deans Marine*

of fittings – usually including propeller shaft(s) and rod and tube from which to make other parts. In this form, the kit manufacturer will very often offer to supply the parts piecemeal as the model is being built, thereby spreading the cost of the build. Although somewhat simpler for the modeller than the basic kit, it still requires some degree of experience.

The third type of kit is the boxed type that contains a pre-made hull, pre-drawn or pre-cut decks, and parts from which to build superstructures. It has detailed and usually illustrated instructions, as well as the necessary fittings, fairleads, bollards, towing gear, etc. – all packaged and carefully listed to make the building of the model as straightforward as possible. Some types of this kit are aimed at the youngster or newcomer and so are excellent starting points for the new ship modeller.

Further up the line, so to speak, come the very

Un-named model tug under construction *Photo courtesy of Mobile Marine*

latest ship models. Those classed, as 'almost ready to run' are complete models, lacking only minimum completion and maybe only needing radio equipment and batteries before they can be tried out on the water. However, there is a variation in quality in some of these (usually) imports from the Far East that makes them to be worthy of close examination before purchase.

Finally, there are the completed and ready-to-run models. As a rule, they are very much more expensive and there is a huge difference between models, according to the builder, the purchase price and the resulting quality. In this category, prices can rise to many thousands of pounds and quite frequently start upwards of £700.00.

Perhaps this is the place to cover, in general terms, the purpose for which the modeller will want the finished vessel. Some will want to sail it for their own pleasure; others will also want to sail it, but in company with other likeminded modellers, some even doing so highly competitively; and some will only wish to place it within a glass case for display purposes. Whichever purpose is chosen or preferred, each will find some help within these pages.

Propulsion methods, steering controls, radio controls or simple fixed steering systems are all listed in later chapters so as to assist the modeller wherever possible.

However, one piece of good advice applicable across the board is always to talk to the staff in the shop or retail outlet. Tell them of your requirements and of your own limitations, as very many retailers are themselves modellers and can offer valuable advice to the prospective builder. Also, join a good model boat club where there is a pond or lake upon which to sail you new model. There, you can join with others and together learn from mistakes.

Finally, take care during building. Certainly, you will make mistakes – everyone makes mistakes – but learn from them and enjoy the build.

Chapter 4

Estuary Tugs and Tug Tenders

The next size up from coastal tug, as it were, in the scale of such vessels, were the estuary tug and tug tender. Originally, these were not necessarily larger than the coastal variety, but were more specialised. In the days of the large liners that made regular ocean voyages to almost exact timetables, there were ports where it was not possible for such a large vessel to berth alongside a quay. The waters may have been too shallow, the terrain similarly difficult, or port facilities may also have been unsuitable for a large vessel and thus berthing could be costly. In these cases, passengers and their often large quantities of luggage were ferried out to and from the liners by tugs

KAPITAN HILGENDORF large tug. *Photo courtesy Deans marine*

IRISHMAN deep sea type tug, model by Model slipway

Left: ENGLISHMAN later model tug by Model Slipway

Below left: CANNING model of preserved steam tug by the author

Right: NEWCASTLE steam tug, by Deans Marine

Below: Admiralty tug (un-named) by Deans Marine

that were especially built to accommodate such loads – that is, in addition to their tug duties of towing.

I often thought of them as attractive vessels, being very similar to a small liner in many ways. At the time of writing, there are only two kits available depicting tug tenders: *Alte Liebe* and *Westbourne*, both by Caldercraft (Jotika). Both are of tugs that were steam driven and were quite small – neither being large enough to ferry passengers out to large liners anchored in the roads off shore. Contrastingly, the larger tenders, such as *Romsey* and *Flying Kestrel* (illustrated in *British Steam Tugs* by Phil Thomas), were fitted with large lounges and saloons for the comfort of the transit passengers.

So, to build models of these passenger-carrying tugs the modeller will need to start from scratch, to seek for and find suitable drawings and to spend time researching details and paint schemes. Research into a particular vessel can be very rewarding and interesting in itself. A great deal of information can be found in the maritime museums, where sensible enquiries can produce valuable data. Nowadays,

too, there is some information to be found on the Internet, although this is more usually confined to modern ships. The library services can also help, as can the plans services of the specialist magazines and specialist marine draughtsmen (see Appendix 2).

In early days, steam tug operators often carried passengers across estuaries and rivers for small fees that served as supplement their main earnings. However, there was no accommodation as such for these passengers and the trips could be hazardous at times. Similarly, some small passenger ships would also carry out towing as a source of extra income. The whole scene was one of fierce competition; it was frequently the first and thus fastest tug to reach the ship needing a tow that gained the fees.

Almost every town close to the sea ran paddle- and screw-steamer excursions of the 'trips round the bay' variety and it was not unusual for tugs used on this service were very heavily and dangerously overloaded.

The tug tender came into its own when passenger liners became too large to go alongside quays in some ports – that is, until serious alterations and dredging

could be carried out.

Thus, it was in the late 1870s that the first two steam tugs were built specifically for the dual purpose of carrying passengers and towing. Notably, most passengers boarding ships in the Clyde were transported by the pleasure steamers that abounded on the river and also sailed to the Scottish Isles. In Ireland, however, at Queenstown and Cobh in Cork, the tug tender was a part of the daily scene. Ships sailing to the U.S.A. from Liverpool, Southampton, etc. called in regularly at the southern ports of Ireland in order to load passengers emigrating to North America.

Some of the large shipping companies had their own tug tenders built. Cunard, for example, commissioned a number of such vessels and a great deal of detail relative to these ships can be found within *British Steam Tugs* by P. N. Thomas and it seems a shame that no kit manufacturer has yet included a tug/tender of the passenger-carrying type such as *Skirmisher*. It was owned by Cunard and, in some respects, resembled an ocean liner, with its wood-topped guard rails and other fine details usually only found on the lager ships of the day.

A great deal of the pleasure of building model ships comes from making a model that is unique and special to one's own. Regrettably, most modellers do not have the time or the facilities to build a model from builder's drawings, nor do they wish to spend valuable time and effort in carrying out extensive research into a particular ship. The kit model provides the quickest way to get a model on the water and, in general, the research work needed has already been carried out by the kit maker before the kit is marketed. However, with a little care and attention, it is possible to adapt the standard kit model and make it unique to the builder. Careful examination of full-size ships and photographs will show where a slight modification has been made during its service life and this can be used to modify the kit model, thereby making it one's own. Often, too, the specific vessel represented in the kit had a sister ship – or even sisters – which were similar but with slight differences. It is such differences that can then can be incorporated into the model to make a related but different ship.

Sometimes it is not possible to find a kit of the specific ship one wishes to build. In these cases, a careful search through the products and supplies of makers who produce hulls of glass reinforced plastic will make it possible to find a hull that has the dimensions needed for the chosen ship. Such a hull, together with the supplied drawings, will often allow the modeller to build the ship of choice. In fact, virtually all of the semi-kit makers are happy to supply their hulls and drawings at fair prices – although, in such cases, there will be no instructions, materials or fittings. The modeller must then create the design and seek out from within the catalogues of the many suppliers the materials that he/she needs. The advantage here, as previously stated, is that this does permit the builder to spread the cost and often get a great deal of enjoyment from solving the many problems that can be encountered in building this way.

Chapter 5

Ocean-going and Salvage Tugs

Ocean-going tugs were an obvious step up from the coastal and river tugs of the early days. Whilst there were some ocean-going paddle tugs, they were no more successful than were the paddle-driven passenger liners of the day. Consequently, development of the steam engine and screw propeller led to the building of the larger tugs expressly for going to sea and providing long distance towing.

The Liverpool tugs *Knights of the Cross* and *Knight of St. John*, built in the late 1800s, were typical ocean-going tugs of their day. They had twin funnels set closely together, were twin-screw driven and reputed to be fine sea ships. Some shipbuilders even specialised in building tugs. Wm. Simons of Renfrew, Redheads at South Shields and Cochrane's of Selby were all regular builders of tugs of all sizes and types,

both steam- and diesel-driven. Once again, the author directs the tug enthusiast to *British Steam Tugs* by P. N. Thomas, now reprinted and available from some of the larger model shops.

The model ocean-going tug or salvage tug is well catered for by the model kit manufacturers. Mobile Marine Models, Model Slipway, Caldercraft and Billings all have salvage tugs in their ranges. The producers of g.r.p. hulls also make hulls of ocean going tugs that can be easily adapted for towing and salvage work and there are many stockists of such hulls. Further, many of the stockists also carry

MOORCOCK a fine large model tug. *Photo courtesy of Ray Brigden*

suitable fittings, which can be used to add detail to the proposed model.

The sort of features to be added are based upon the fact that the majority of large, sea-going tugs depend more upon large towing winches than upon tow hooks, although hooks are still to be found and used on such ships. The automatic towing winch is, as previously mentioned, usually set beneath an overhanging deck in order to provide a degree of protection in heavy weather.

Such winches are capable of carrying considerable lengths of towing hawser, over nearly 2 km or a mile in many cases. Steel wire, however, is inflexible and means that suitable shock-absorbing equipment is fitted to take the strains of towing from a stop. The winches let out the tow rope to a suitable length when towing in deep water and an ocean-going tug towing a dead ship over a long voyage can often use a tow rope length of about a kilometre (half-a-mile) or more. The precise reason for using a long-distance tow is believed to be that it reduces tension over the relative length, provides grater elasticity and is therefore less likely to snap.

Left: Large model tug by Deans marine

Below left: AYTON CROSS large tug model by the author

Right: Stern deck detail of AYTON CROSS model

Large tugs of this pattern frequently carried out duties other than simple towing and they carried a great deal of equipment specifically for salvage work. Initially, crew accommodation was fully enclosed, most passages being enclosed as protection from inclement weather. In addition, there were often a number of spare cabins for the use of personnel who may have been rescued and needed to be taken ashore quickly. In recent years, however, virtually all such accommodation has become heated and air-conditioned, allowing the tug to work in a range of temperatures and sea conditions, from tropical waters to the polar seas.

Design problems became apparent in the need for a salvage tug need to get to a vessel in distress quickly, because high speed does not equate to the high bollard pull needed for towing purposes. A compromise was almost the only answer and that is evident in the use of twin screws being allied to fair speed. So, whilst ocean-going and salvage tugs rarely use the Voith Schneider unit or the azimuthing propeller system, they are very often fitted with bow and stern thrusters athwartships in order to give greater manoeuvrability at slow speeds. However, the bow and stern thrusters fitted in this manner are not effective if the vessel is moving forward or backward at more than a dead slow speed, when the water passes the ports without entering them and encountering the thruster screws,

A deep-sea and salvage tug is, of necessity, a large vessel and is often longer than 200 feet (about 60 m) in length. It carries portable equipment, such as air compressors, powered pumps and similar machinery that can be lifted aboard the damaged ship to assist the ship's own pumps, etc. when necessary. To handle such sizeable equipment, all such vessels have substantial, hydraulically operated cranes with a long reach. Other equipment carried includes collision mats, welding gear, lifejackets, and life rafts in canisters, medical supplies and all other items needed to assist in rescuing any personnel involved in a damaged ship. The most modern of these tugs even have a helicopter pad built into the ship to permit landings and take off when extra equipment or personnel are needed, or to carry a damaged person quickly ashore to the nearest hospital.

Possibly one of the most lucrative types of operation for the large-ocean going tug is salvage work. High fees are paid for the successful salvage of a large vessel that can be brought back into service. Equally large fees are payable for the salvage of cargo and personnel – that is, if the cargo then reaches its port undamaged and in good condition, whilst the value of life is, of course, incalculable.

The modeller wishing to build an ocean-going and/or salvage tug should always seek out as much information as possible relative to the chosen ship. Salvage machinery loaded on deck can be simulated or shown packaged in a crate. With the latter choice, a simple box of fine timber will suffice and is then shown as being securely tied down and possibly covered in tarpaulin.

It is very satisfying to make the model's details as accurate and realistic as is possible. In checking such matters, have found today's ship owners to be particularly helpful if approached sensibly. Most tug owners are extremely proud of their ships and are only too pleased to show them to the keen modeller who can, perhaps to confirm credibility and depth of interest, show photographs of previously built models. The author is more than fortunate to have access to both ship yard, docks and ship owners near his home and his camera is in operation on an almost daily business.

The modeller should be aware that the larger the model, then the more complex it will be and have a serious bearing upon the cost. Modern materials for glass fibre hulls, resins for casting and white metals have increased in cost substantially in recent times and so the outlay for a large kit can reach as high as four figures in pounds sterling. However, some makers – such as Mobile Marine Models – do offer a package deal on their larger models, whereby the kit outfit can be bought in separate sections at the time and enabling the modeller to spread the costs over the period of building the ship. Alternatively, some modellers will, of course, spread their costs by using a credit or debit card with those manufacturers who can provide credit facilities.

There are another financial aspects to this type of modelling that are often overlooked. So, the wisest modellers will ensure that their models are insured once completed and shown as separate items on the household policy. After all, a fine model can be very valuable and very difficult to replace and/or repair, should such unfortunate circumstances arise.

Furthermore, the prospective model builder should also be aware that a large, complicated model can occupy a great many hours of construction time, particularly if all tools and materials have to be stored away after each building session.　Working to a fairly easy daily programme of 6 to 8 hours, the author generally finds that it takes from 300 hours upwards for scratch building a reasonably sized ship; and possibly as many as 200 hour even if building up a good quality kit. These figures are for guidance only and so the average modeller might expect to take some time longer. Nevertheless, if these times are equated to spare time, evenings and weekends, then a 10-hour week becomes a 30-week build – more than half a year.

One will gather that a great deal of time has been spent covering the kit model and little has been said of the model built entirely from scratch – but this is rectified in the forthcoming chapters. Some may find that the information given in these first chapters is not new – and to some extent this is true. However, such

YORKSHIREMAN sister ship to IRISHMAN illustrated on page 25

data is of value and this book is directed not only to the modeller of existing ability, but also to the newcomer who may know little or nothing of the tug and its duties. Furthermore, the modeller, whether new or experienced, will very soon realise that they need to become masters of more than one trade. They must be shipwrights of a kind, engineers in a small way, joiners and cabinet makers, painters and decorators – as well electricians and radio engineers to cap all off. The building of a model tug is all-absorbing and those who do delve into this hobby will discover real enjoyment. For those who build models to sail, they will have many happy times upon the lake; those who build for display will gain happy hours looking at their work; and for those who build to compete with others comes the excitement of the contest. Ship modelling is a fine hobby and is open to all.

Chapter 6

Small Tugs and Towing

There are many kinds of small tugs used within the confines of the world's rivers, harbours and canals. Many of these tugs are specifically designed for the service they provide. For example, whilst rarely seen in the U.K., the pusher tug is used widely on the major rivers of the U.S.A. for handling trains of barges from astern. It usually operates with barges linked together in pairs and close-coupled. The tug then pushes the train, steering from the stern. Tugs like these invariably have a heavy framework of steel and timber at the bow in order to accept the loading. At the time of writing, the author knows of no kits being produced of such a vessel, although the plans services do have drawings available (see Appendix 2). In addition, some enterprising U.K. modellers have

successfully built and operated pusher tugs.

For many years, the barge-handling tugs on the River Thames have been of the towing kind. In early days, they were steam driven and coal fired – and their funnels and masts were arranged to be lowered to allow passage through the low bridges that up river of Tower Bridge. Today, the average small tug on the Thames is powered by a diesel engine and carries a very short funnel. The bridges above Tower Bridge are all too low to allow a merchant ship of reasonable size to reach bank-side warehouses upstream and until not

WILANNE small tug model – ideal for novice builder.
Photo courtesy of Mobile Marine

Detail of bow of pusher tug. *Photo by Mobile Marine*

so long ago, such vessels discharged their cargoes on to barges in the main docks and the small barge tugs carried the cargoes to their final destination and vice versa. The Thames bargeman trade became traditional with whole families involved in the business.

A good example of a river tug in kit form is *Riverman* from the Caldercraft range (see Appendix 2), which makes up into an attractive model, either built statically or fully working under radio control. *Riverman* is a single screw, conventially driven tug, whereas many modern tugs are driven by Schottel or Voith Schneider units, often with two or more such units to give a high degree of manoeuvrability. In more recent times, it has been noted that a number of tugs are now being fitted with their drive equipment forward of amidships, particularly when they are fitted with Voith Schneider or similar propulsion units. With the drive units located forward of the centre of the tug, the engines are drawing the vessel along instead of pushing. It is believed that this increases manoeuvrability.

These types of drive equipment are becoming increasingly popular with tug designers, as they permit the tug to exert its bollard pull with ease and in almost any direction. Graupner, Robbe and Marx Luder in Germany all produce model Schottel drives and azimuthing units to a single scale size and, to date, there is no indication that alternative sizes will be produced. Very recently, however, Graupner has started to market a kit of parts from which Voith Schneider drives may be constructed – but, regrettably, only to the single scale of 1:32.

Handling barges in both tidal and confined waters demands a high degree of skill that is only gained by many years of working in the business. It is probable that the pusher tug handles its barges more easily than does the towing tug as, in effect, the closely coupled barges and the tug become a single unit. A tug towing a barge train has more problems than one which pushed since the tug master has to consider how to stop the train – there are no brakes – as well as how it is to be steered. When towing, any sudden stop or severe slowing by the tug can easily cause the barges to overrun the tug with disastrous consequences – and it is not unknown for a tug and its entire crew to be lost due to an overrunning barge train. Skilful handling and quick reactions by the tug master will generally avoid such problems. But what usually saves the day is the anticipation of the problem before it occurs.

The usual complement of a small river tug is three men; the tug master, the engineman and a deckhand. Sometimes a boy or apprentice learning the business supplements this crew. There is also usually one man on board the towed barge train whose job it is to help with steering and to lengthen or shorten the tow rope as required.

Successful towing of a model tug often depends upon how the tow is 'roped up'. It is a mistake to have the leading tug use a long tow line. This can cause a serious delayed reaction when turning. Rather, it is much safer to have a short tow, so that turns can be effective and accurate. Similarly, it is best to

TID classic wartime tug. Model by Deans Marine

'rope' the stern tug on to the tow so that maximum thrust can be used to brake and slow down the barge train. Practice on the part of the model tug master is the real answer to becoming expert at model tug handling. Un full service, tugs handling large ships in confined waters such as river or canal will invariably couple closely to the tow. In this way they can turn the tow accurately and ensure that the tow remains within the navigable area of the waters. On the other hand, if the tow is ocean-going and the tug is hauling over a long distance, then the tow hawser will usually be very long – about a kilometer or half-a-mile in some cases.

A real danger of which to be aware for both in full-size service or with the model tug is the chance of the tug becoming 'beam on' to the tow. When this happens, the tug is drawn sideways and can sometimes be capsized. In real life, prompt action by the tug master will avoid such dangers – and so the modeller should also be aware of this danger. In general, model tugs are valuable to their owners, so that accidents should be anticipated and avoided at all costs.

A further consideration for the model tug master is the composition of the tow rope itself. This should always be made or spun from a material that has a degree of flexibility – so that it will act as a spring when the tug takes up the tow, particularly if the tow is lying dead in the water. Power applied to a tow through a steel rope without any 'give' can easily tear

the tow hook (or towing winch) clean away from the model, also damaging the deck and superstructure. Remember too that when handling large ships, full-size tugs always proceed slowly and move with care. This is done so that there will be little chance of the tow taking control and running away by its sheer weight. By sheer momentum, a 50,000-ton/tonne deadweight oil tanker takes a great deal of stopping once it begins to move!

The small tugs used for barge handling or for harbour duty have substantial belts of timber or rubber faced steel round their hulls to protect them from damage when working, docking, or from running alongside a pushing or pulling tow. Huge rope-made protective cushions, known as Turk's Head fenders, were the usual form of protection for the bows and sterns. Most good model shops stock model rope fenders in a range of sizes; and some kit manufacturers include small miniature car/lorry tyres within their kits from which to make the fender most commonly seen today. In fact, almost all working tugs are ringed by a series of old lorry tyres for protective purposes. The most modern of small tugs also have a strong steel frame attached to the bow and faced in heavy timber expressly to allow the tug to push another vessel with safety.

A excellent source of information and photographs of working vessels, tugs and cargo ships is to be found within the pages of the magazines *Sea Breezes, Ships Monthly* and *Shipping Today* and *Yesterday*. Most of these are available from the larger newsagent's shops – and can, of course, be obtained on subscription. One publication only recently examined in any detail

FURIE model of vintage tug tender by Deans Marine

by the author is the periodical *Ships in Focus Record*. The issues are of high quality and each deals with a selected number of marine subjects. For example a section will be devoted to a given shipping company, one to a certain ship, one to some marine casualty of note, etc. At the time of writing, Issue No. 40 is the latest I have seen, but copies of all the previous editions are available and the publishers do provide a catalogue of each issue's contents. Its publishers are John & Marion Clarkson of Preston (see Appendix 2). The maritime museums can often provide information and photographs of specific ships; and sometimes they can also produce copies of the selected ship's drawings.

Enquiries among ship owners, in the author's experience has been productive and most owners are proud of their fleets and willing to help the genuine modeller with information when it is available. Letters to marine museums do seem to take longer for replies to be received, but a visit to such a place will more likely prove productive. It goes without saying that all requests of this nature should be couched in polite terms and, where a letter is sent requesting information, common courtesy demands the inclusion of a pre-paid return addressed envelope.

The keen modeller will spend some time on researching his/her chosen ship and such research can be pleasurable and interesting. Visits to ports and riverside berths are far from easy these days. However, it is possible, on some occasions, to obtain a permit to make a visit. Such a port visit with a good camera will pay dividends to the keen modeller. Good models can only be built, even from kits, by researching into the vessel's background and history and ensuring that the model is built to the date of the research.

Since the 1980s, there has been a growing tendency for tugs to use the more exotic types of propulsion, such as the azimuthing propeller unit and the Voith Schneider unit. Single-screw tugs are becoming rare; and at the time of writing, the author knows of no single-screw tug under construction anywhere. The majority of small tug designers favour the azimuthing or Voith Schneider units, many variations can be seen. In sequence, the most common are the twin azimuthing units mounted astern, followed by a similar arrangement but with the units forward of the main superstructure – tractor drive – and twin Voith Schneider units with one aft and the other forward. There is also a tendency to prefer tractor drive where the drive units are mounted forward and a large skeg is fitted aft. Some of these tractor pattern tugs have recently been built with twin azimuthing units forward and one aft.

The model press and magazines such as *Ships Monthly* are reliable sources of information as to such developments. However, as such units need to be 'home' built, but just how effective these well-made model azimuthing units perform in service is yet to be accurately assessed. The Voith Schneider units made by Graupner are described later and the author knows of at least one model with these installed and that performs well (although not yet observed in towing duty). The prospective model tug master can be spoilt for choice and so needs to select his/her project with due care and attention.

Materials

Model ships can be built from a wide variety of materials. However, listed and discussed within this chapter are most of the materials that are suitable for such modelling. Even though they would, of course, appear in high-quality models of luxury yachts and passenger vessels, the more exotic timbers – such as mahogany, teak and walnut – have but little use in the building of a model tug and so are not listed in any detail here. It should be born in mind that the working ship (tug) is invariably painted, so that whichever material is used to form its shapes, all will be covered eventually with some coloured paint – and the basic material will be effectively disguised. The paint on the model needs to be well applied, of good quality and pleasing finish. Full details of painting and finishing a model are to be found in Chapter 14.

Tin plate

In earlier years, most model ships were built from tin plate over timber or brass frames, much in the same way that a full-size ship is plated. Such material is not difficult to handle and, when clean, easy to solder and secure to suitable frames. Unfortunately, tin plate will corrode easily if it is not carefully treated and then painted. Shaping the plate to the complex curves of the ship is also difficult and it is a material that does not lend itself to easy. So, because metalworking does indeed require considerable specialist skill and requires careful treatment in order to preserve it, tin plate models seem to have almost completely disappeared

Card and pasteboard

Scale model ships, even tugs, can be built from cardboard or pasteboard. It is a flexible and clean material that can easily be rendered waterproof by the application of successive coatings of cellulose dope. This stiffens and seals the card and is followed by a number of coats of approved paint and varnish.

The hull of the working ship model needs to be fairly strong and a keel of plywood or similar timber will be necessary to reinforce the card-built model. Card in itself is not really substantial enough from which to build a working model tug that will have to handle odd and heavy conditions during its working life.

A great deal of patience is needed to shape card and pasteboard to the curves of the tug – so its use should be restricted to places where it will be cosmetically of advantage. However, although not a model of a tug, there is a kit on the market that replicates a standard SD14 cargo ship and which is built entirely from card. It follows a standard, welded ship pattern in construction and is 2 m (almost 80 inches) long when completed – a project for the strong-minded and very patient model ship builder.

Plywood

This is probably the most commonly used material from which to build a model tug from scratch. As a result, many model ships and tugs are made entirely from fine marine-quality plywood in various thicknesses. This type of good quality plywood is produced in Finland, Russia and Sweden, and is sold in small quantities by most model stores and kit makers. It is available in thicknesses of 0.4, 0.8, 1.0, 1.5, 2.0, 3.0, 4.0, and 6.0 mm and in sheets of up to 1500 mm square – although ply can be bought for making keels and beams, where a heavy construction

Four sizes of birch plywood – 0.8, 1.5, 3.0 and 6.0 mm thick

Sample of Jelutong timber in block form

is needed. Most model shops will also sell their plywood stocks in smaller sheet sizes as a matter of convenience, most such sheets being about 30 cm (12 inches) wide.

A very useful specialist plywood is 'Liteply' which is soft and freely worked. It is used mainly for flying type model aircraft but is also very suitable for the construction of deckhouses and superstructures, its light weight reducing the possibility of a capsize due to top weight. However, its light and open grain does need careful treatment and it needs to be well sealed before any paint is applied. In configuration, it is – in effect – two layers of thin birch timber enclosing a layer of balsa and all secured by a high quality adhesive.

Balsa

Although technically classed as a hardwood, balsa is a soft, readily carved and shaped timber. It is ideal for making the blocks that may be wanted to shape the bow and stern section of a complex hull shape, where it would be difficult to apply harder timber planks. The wood is a very open grained and almost knot-free, although the very soft nature of its composition seems at odds with its classification. Although very easy to work, it needs razor-sharp tools when cutting across the grain and in order to avoid quite serious flaking round the edges of the cut.

Most model shops stock balsa in block and sheet form, so that it can be used for the complete building of small ship models. However, it needs to have a good grain filler applied in order to create a suitable surface for the subsequent paint. Sanding is easy, but the soft surface is very easily marked and thus such smoothing should be used with care. For example, if the bows of a model made from balsa strike another ship – say, when handling a larger vessel – then, almost certainly, the balsa area will be damaged and need repair.

Jelutong

More suitable than balsa, but used in the same manner, is the knot-free wood known as jelutong. It is appreciably harder than balsa and used extensively by pattern makers because of its knot-free properties and the ease with which it can be worked, carved and cut. It is not as easily marked, as is balsa and is ideal for the making of bow and stern blocks for the model tug. It can also be turned in a lathe and carved to make fine shapes for window surrounds, etc. Although not so easily found, it can be bought from a few selected suppliers (see Appendix 2). The author uses jelutong for making a number of small parts such as warping drums for winches, etc. The wood holds up well to fine turning and shaping and is to be recommended.

Miscellaneous woods

The more exotic timbers have already been mentioned at the start of the chapter, but there are others that can prove useful to the scratch builder. Obeche, in thin strips, is suitable for planking the hull and or decks of a model. It tends to be brittle and will need to be steamed or soaked before it will bend without breaking. Birch as found in good marine plywood is an ideal planking timber. It has few knots, and in strip form is very flexible, with a fine-grained surface that accepts paint and fillers readily. Similarly, lime is also a fine planking material for the timber hull.

All of the above can be found in both sheet, strip and block form from specialist suppliers. However, the more exotic timber, the costlier it will be. Although the decks of most ships were made from teak, in full size practice, deal is much more common on the tug. But teak, even in small quantities, is not easy to use. It is open grained and oily, requiring a fair degree of surface attention to seal and prepare it for paint or varnish.

Consequently, it is much easier to simulate deck planks using birch or thin birch plywood, where the light colour is much closer to the bleached teak found on board the real ship. For models built on the 'bread and butter' fashion (explained later) planks of English lime or basswood, etc. are ideal. Such planks need to be planed truly flat and preferably to the thickness commensurate with the ship's line drawings. Thinner strips of the same timbers may also be used for deck planking, etc.

In truth, the scale tug modeller really does not need much by way of exotic wood and most tasks can be carried out with the more common timbers. For making masts and derricks, the modeller will find birch dowel ideal. It can be found in various diameters in most model shops and is often of birch, but lime dowel and some of the hard woods such as walnut and mahogany can also be found. For mast construction, the dowel will need to be tapered and this can be successfully done by sanding.

Boxwood is an Ideal timber from which to make small and detailed parts. It is very hard but very suitable for turning, easily sanded to a very smooth surface and can be waxed and polished to a high gloss when necessary. It does, of course, accept paints easily and gives a smooth surface for the paint. Whilst it is fairly expensive, even in small quantities as small blocks and planks, it is well worth having a small quantity in stock.

Styrene sheet

The material that has come into the most common use among model ship builders in recent years has been polystyrene in sheet form (sometimes erroneously called 'plasticard'). It is available in a variety of thicknesses from 0.5 to 2.5 mm. and in sheets up to 1500 x 1000 mm in area. It is a hard plastic, generally white in colour, that gives a fine surface for paint and which is readily glued together with liquid polystyrene cement. When heated, it can be moulded and shaped and it is used frequently in vacuum-moulding machines to produce repeat identical copies of a given part or pattern. It is easily cut with a sharp knife and can be snapped along a line scored by a knife. The edges sand freely and smoothly and the material can be trimmed to quite complex curves or to follow uneven shapes. Lastly, the material is impervious to water and some other liquids and is ideal from which to make deckhouses and other details for the model tug.

Liquid polystyrene cement can be applied with a small brush to a joint held together in the hand when the liquid will be drawn into the joint by capillary action and sealing quite quickly. The joined parts can be handled after only a few minutes, but the full bonded strength will not be reached in much under 12 hours from application. Thus, it is always wise to allow the adhesive a reasonable time to cure before sanding and preparing the material for further work.

Styrene can be found in many useful shapes, such as tube, angle, rod, etc., and most good model shops will stock these shapes in various sizes produced under the proprietary names of 'Plastruct' or 'Evergreen'. These pre-shaped forms are invaluable to the tug modeller as they can be used in many places on the model. Although they seem to have been produced with the railway or architectural model in mind, they certainly do have their uses in the model marine world.

Glass reinforced plastics (GRP)

Objects made from glass reinforced plastics can be found in almost every home, workplace, garage, etc. throughout the country. Known generally as GRP (sometimes g.r.p.), it is used extensively for the manufacture of model ship hulls where a master mould is made from a carefully made plug and wherein the liquid material and woven glass cloth can be married to harden into the form of the previously removed plug. Not only are the hulls of model ships made from GRP, but deckhouses, funnels and similar structures are often moulded to suit the given model or kit.

In the raw state, the material comprises a liquid resin to which is added a catalyst that initiates the hardening process. To add strength to the proposed shape, loosely woven glass cloth is embedded in the resin as it is brushed or sprayed into the mould. The commonest type of resin is polyester and it is usually purchased in activated form, requiring the addition of the catalyst to start the chemical reaction. The resin has a pungent smell and needs care when used in the liquid state – when it can be treated to render it heat resistant to a certain degree, making it suitable for the hull that has to carry a steam plant.

In its solid state, it is easily worked and can be drilled, tapped, sawn, and sanded, providing a first class surface for the application of paint. In this solid state, it is impervious to water and resistant to oil.

Chapter 9 gives further details of the use of GRP in model tug building. However, there are more expensive forms of GRP, such as those made from epoxy compounds and those that have the addition of carbon fibre or Teflon fibres to impart greater strength. Use of such compounds is generally restricted to the making of fine, high-speed model yachts and power boats, where a light but strong hull is vital. Frankly, the expense of the more exotic resins is not really justified when making a model tug or similar ship.

Other materials

The materials described above are those most commonly used in building model ships, but there are many other materials that have their use, even if they are only used in very small quantities.

Brass and stainless steel are needed for propeller shafts, and brass or bronze are needed for the propeller. Brass strip and angle also have their uses, as does sheet brass that can be used as bought or etched to produce guard rail stanchions and similar small necessities. Aluminium tube and rod can be used in selected places; and copper wire, tube and sheet is easily worked and can be a useful material in selected places on the model.

Very useful, too, is the material known as white metal, a soft, tin-based material that melts at fairly low temperatures and can poured into a prepared mould to give repeated, identical parts. Kits are available for making such moulds of silicon rubber and include small slabs of the white metal and small crucibles in which to melt the material. These allow the modeller to produce a number of identical parts from a single, well-made master. The operation is comparatively simple to carry out and well within the

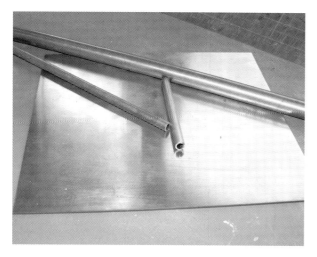

Brass sheet, tube and bar such as would be found in a modeller's workshop.

500 m.litre can of liquid poly cement – bulk purchase in this case, as it is usually sold in small bottles.

powers of the average tug modeller.

In similarly made moulds, it is also possible to cast parts in resins and a number of model kit makers include resin parts within the fittings kits for their models. Such parts have the advantage of being of light in weight and thus limit the top weight of, say, a model tender to a sensible level.

Much more in standard use today than even a few years ago are the small fittings etched in brass or nickel plate. A number of kit makers include etched fittings within their kits and there are other makers who specialise in the provision of etched fittings. Such etched fittings are available in a variety of scales so that the ship modeller is well served. The material is easily cut from the brass or nickel plate sheet and needs little preparation to accept paints and varnishes. Where very small scale parts are needed, items such as guard rails are etched in strips. For larger rails, the stanchions are etched complete with the necessary holes through which the horizontal wires can be run.

The materials detailed above have all been tried and tested many times by the author and many other modellers, where their uses have been found to advantage. However, all materials should be handled carefully and should not be employed on a model until the modeller feels comfortable with their use. Also, remain aware that cleanliness is vital for any material to accept paint of almost any kind and some materials benefit from the application of an etching primer before the chosen colours can be applied. Thus, is it is always wise to check the surface condition before applying paint.

Adhesives

The range of adhesives available today is so wide and varied that the modeller can easily be led up the wrong path. Many modern adhesives have their uses within the modelling scene and it those proven to be the most suitable that are described here. Some model

makers will have experience of alternatives and will continue to use their own glues. It remains everyone's option to select a suitable adhesive for a certain job and, if one happy with it, continue to use it.

For joining timber to timber, and timber derivatives, the most used glue is PVA. (polyvinyl acetate) a thick, white creamy glue. It dries both clear and hard and allows for a fairly short initial cure time. It is available as a standard woodworking adhesive and also as a water-resistant compound known as aliphatic glue, the latter is being preferred for assembling timber hulls. It is readily available from tool stores, large super store outlets and all good model shops. It comes under a number of proprietary brand names, but most are almost identical in composition. It is an adhesive that should always find space on the workshop shelf.

For joining timber to GRP or to styrene (and as a standby to PVA adhesive) two-part epoxy resin glue is very useful. This adhesive comes in two parts that need to be mixed together before application. The process of mixing initiates a chemical reaction that hardens the mixture and effects the joint. It comes in a few forms too, the first being a 'quick grab' type that is both fast and reliable but unsuitable for immersion in water. The second is the two-hour type, with a slower reaction and thereby more time to align parts to be joined. It is hard and solid when completely

Typical super glue (cyano acrylate with accelerator.

when working with styrene sheet and styrene parts. Liquid polystyrene cement is available from most good model shops and is produced by a number of manufacturers under their own brand names There is little to choose between them and the modeller should try them and select the one that he/she considers best.

Using the above cement, it is also possible to create a styrene surface on a piece of plywood if one first applies two or three coats of cement and allows each coat to dry. A piece of thin styrene sheet can then be attached to the plywood using the same cement, where it will bond to the timber and become almost impossible to remove.

In the past, joining metal to alternate materials has been problematic until the advent of 'Superglue' (cyanoacrylate glue). It has become extremely popular over recent years and it is now available in a number of types. A very rapidly curing material, it will effectively join human skin to almost any material and this could be a serious problem at one time. However, the experts found a release agent so that firmly glued-together fingers can now be a thing the past. Cyano comes in liquid form and generally of three types (speeds). The thinnest is the fastest to cure and needs mere fractions of seconds to become effective. The medium type is slower running and thus provides a short period of time for repositioning if necessary. The thickest (almost jelly) is the slowest the strongest and maybe easiest to use. However, it takes some time to cure but can be speeded up by the use of an accelerator spray. As with other adhesives, cyano needs to be used in a well-ventilated atmosphere. As the name indicates, it is a material containing cyanide and is therefore poisonous. Ideal for the gluing of metal parts to other materials, it extensively used for attaching unlike materials to each other and with almost complete success. With wide-grained materials such as soft woods, balsa, etc., it is wise to pre-coat the gluing area with a thin coating of the cyano and allow it to dry before making the joint conventionally with the same glue.

Attaching veneers to timber surfaces, or even to styrene surfaces, requires the use of a contact adhesive such as Durofix or Evostik. In recent years, the latter has been modified to remove its aromatic fumes – with their pungent smell and potentially addictive property – and it now often sold complete with a small sponge applicator. As with all contact adhesives, both surfaces to be joined need to be thinly coated with the glue and allowed to become tack dry (touch dry), whereupon when they are brought together they will bond instantly. Because of this, accurate location is essential as there is only one chance to get it right. The bond is made so rapidly that there is rarely any time for repositioning, although a two to three hours should be allowed for the joint to become fully cured.

cured, though doubtful for use under water. The third and final is 24-hour type; and whilst it is the slowest to cure, is waterproof when cured and best used for securing parts such as propeller shafts to hulls. In general, epoxy adhesives need fairly warm conditions for them to cure and allow evacuation of the volatile gases that are released in the process. Epoxy glues are also suitable for attaching small metal parts to timber, styrene and GRP. It is always wise, though, to roughen the area of the joint where the glue is to be applied.

Styrene sheet is best joined using a polystyrene cement. Tubes of this can be bought but the glue is prone to stringing and is not easy to place precisely where it is needed – but holding two parts together while applying liquid polystyrene from a small brush is relatively easy and quick. Such a joint will be firm enough to leave after only a few moments, although full strength will take up to 10 hours. As with the epoxy and resin glues, liquid polystyrene cement works by chemical reaction and time is needed for the volatile gases to escape. As these fumes can be unpleasant, the cement should always be used in a ventilated atmosphere. But these are only minor drawbacks and there is no real substitute

Chapter 8

Tools and Equipment

For any newcomer to model tug building, it is a fallacy to imagine that general or household tools are adequate for modelling. They really will not do the job. Model ships, particularly tugs, are fairly small units – so large pistol drills and hammers, rip saws and panel saws are almost always far too large for the small jobs. Instead, the keen modeller will build up a tool kit especially for modelling use. Such a kit will and can be quite small to begin with, but should be bought sensibly with a view to expansion of the hobby over time.

Of course, much will depend upon where the modeller is to build his/her model. Often, the only available home space is the kitchen table or, if one is lucky, a spare bedroom. Of the two, the latter is preferable as it could be possible to leave unfinished work on the worktop overnight or even untouched for a few days – whereas the kitchen would have to be cleared following each modelling session. Some modellers are fortunate enough to have garden shed large enough to use as a workshop, while others will use a section of their garage. In both cases, the working space should be rendered as damp proof as possible and given a degree of insulation – and a small heater for cosiness in winter is also a sensible purchase for such spaces.

A solid top bench is a real asset, though an old pine table – even if purchased second-hand – can be sanded smooth and serve well as a work bench, especially if the legs are well braced and fixed firmly. A small vice screwed or clamped to the bench is also useful. Finally, the top of the bench should be protected from undue scratches – maybe by a covering of clean linoleum or similarly tough material. A so-called 'self-healing' cutting mat that is made specially for the purpose of scoring and cutting fine or thin materials saves damaging knife blade points and stops the knife wander off course when cutting. Such mats can be found in craft shops, model stores and good stationery outlets stores. They are relatively inexpensive and can be bought in a number of sizes that relate to the equivalent standard metric paper formats of as A4, A3, and A2.

Steel squares useful, in the small sizes, for modelling purposes.

Hand tools

The first hand tool to be considered is a good craft knife. It should be firm and comfortable to hold and use – and one that accepts snap-off blades is ideal for model work. Remember: always buy the very best tools you can afford; cheap tools rarely last, they lose their edge and frequently fail right in the middle of that important job.

The second purchase should be a quality steel rule, preferably of stainless steel and well marked in both imperial and metric scales. A 300-mm/12-inch steel rule can be used as secure knife guide in addition to marking off measurements when cutting thin sheet. A small engineer's square, also of stainless steel, is also a wise purchase. These come usually in sizes of 50, 75 and 100 mm (or in 2, 3 and 4 inches), with the 50-mm or 3-inch version possibly the most useful of the range.

With these three tools one can actually start to build a fine model from a kit but for more detailed work and for building from scratch, the modeller will need a number of additional tools. (Please note that up to now, none of these can be said to be unduly costly, although one does need to pay a little more for high quality).

For cutting sheet plywood and some thin planks of timber, a fretsaw frame with a selection of blades is a boon. Also, a small, 50-g or 2-ounce ball pein hammer is ideal for driving small fine pins into timber. Other requirements include a pair of sharp

A selection of clamps – all are valuable additions to the workshop, the small spring pattern being particularly useful.

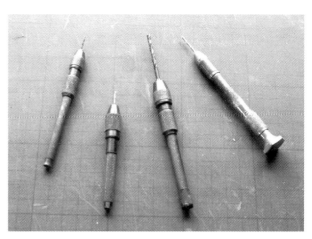

Small pin vices are valuable for holding tiny drills to make small holes in odd places.

scissors – and a good pencil will obviously be needed. For drilling, a small hand drill with a range of bits will be adequate for most modelling jobs. Finally, for smoothing timber surfaces, a small plane (known as a David plane) is good value and obtainable from a range of outlets.

An essential item of workshop equipment is a truly flat surface. Most large engineering works employed large, cast iron tables, the surface of which was ground and polished to be truly and very accurately flat.

Castings and other items of machinery that needed to be machined, drilled or milled were placed upon this table and, using sharp scribers, they were marked off for accurate drilling, grinding, etc. Obviously, the model work place is usually too small and the pocket will not stretch to allow the purchase of such an accurate piece of equipment. However there is an alternative, in that a sheet of plate glass serves well as a surface plate.

Scrap pieces of such material can often be bought cheaply from the local glazier, though it should be free of surface scratches and of a fair thickness, and – of course – it must be quite flat. Before us, it should be well cleaned with warm water and detergent, and examined for any blemishes that would negate its use. It should then be dried with a soft cloth and lightly polished, as one would clean a window. Used on the flat top of the bench, repeated measurements taken from it to the workpiece will be consistent and accurate. Such a piece of glass need only measure 300 sq. mm (or 12 x 12 inches) or so – and once bought, should be stored carefully between periods of use.

Reverting to the small hammer and its use, always

This selection of small hand tools is a good base from which to build up a tool kit for model making, there is almost all that is initially needed.

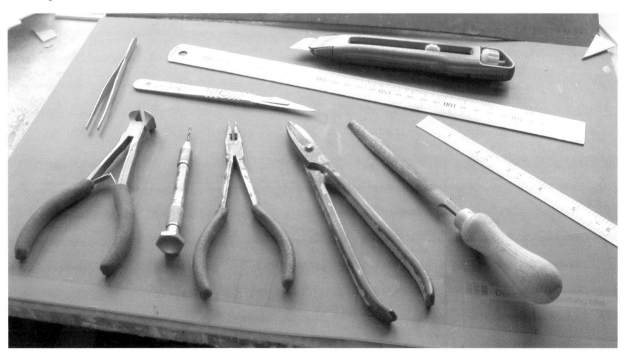

ensure that the head is kept polished. During use, it will invariably gain a coating of glue or dirt that needs to be polished away. Many a fine brass pin has been bent and rendered useless by a dirty hammer head. Also, no one strikes a pin or nail precisely. Almost always, as the hammer strikes, the head is travelling slightly sideways, So, when the head is dirty, it drags the pin and bends it – a small but valuable point that has been proven in the author's workshop on many occasions. Holding small pins manually in order to allow them to be driven into the workpiece is almost impossible, as fingers are not pointed or small enough. However, a pair of long-nosed pliers 125-150 mm (or 5-6 inches) long) are ideal for this job and they will be useful for many other tasks too. There will be little need for larger pliers, although a pair with standard jaws and/or that offer side cutting will be found useful.

To complement the function of pliers, the modeller should consider one or two good quality sets of tweezers. A pair with sharp points can be used for many small tasks; and tweezers of the locking blade pattern can also be very useful. Tweezers like these are frequently sold in sets of four or five, offering alternative blade shapes, so such a set could prove a wise purchase.

Moving on to slightly larger tools, the wood chisel has to be mentioned. Good chisels are always expensive, and are often sold in sets of three or four and of varying widths. For the modeller who uses timber and plywood in preference to other materials, a set of good chisels will be a wise purchase. They need to be kept sharp and the blades should be protected when stored. Practice in keeping a keen edge comes with experience, an oilstone of two grits is needed and the beginner would possibly be wise to buy either a guide tool or to seek assistance from a more experience person. Always remember that it is not the sharp tool that slips and cuts the hand, but the blunt one that needs so much extra force that causes the damage.

Some makers, such as Exacto, produce boxed sets of modelling tools comprising craft knife handles, replaceable blades, a sanding block and often a small plane. There is often also a small saw blade that will fit one of the craft knife handles. As with other sharp edged tools, the blade of the plane must be kept sharp if it is to do the job for which it was designed. Sanding blocks need not form part of the purchase of tools, they can be simply made from scraps of plywood and timber – and if the abrasive paper it attached only at either end, then it can be readily changed as needed. A number of such sanding blocks, each with a different grade of abrasive, will always be useful.

The range of abrasive papers and cloths available today is very wide indeed. The model tug maker will need some for smoothing surfaces, shaping corners and curves, etc. The abrasives based on aluminium oxide are the cheapest and easiest to buy, and grits of 80, 120 and 200 will suffice; but for very fine surface finishing and to smooth away blemishes in paintwork, 'wet and dry' papers are the best to use. These also range in grit and 180, 400, 600 and even 1200 grits will be found useful. When treating timber, only use 'wet and dry' paper in a dry mode. Used wet. it will raise the grain of the wood and create more work rather than less.

Finally, a small screwdriver or two will be needed. A model ship will quite often need to have screws to hold parts together, where the part held needs to be easily removed, and so a screwdriver of the right type is essential. Nowadays, these also come in boxed sets, offering alternate heads to accommodate the varying tops of the modern screw.

(Where a great deal of information is repeated here or from previous sources, be assured that it is repeated because of the value the author places upon such information and data. It is hoped that it will be appreciated in the same spirit that it is given.)

Power tools

A workshop fully equipped with lathe, pedestal drill, milling machine, powered saws, air compressor and large working surfaces is, sadly, only a dream for most tug modellers. However, a comprehensive range of tools and equipment can be built up over time, particularly if one buys wisely and takes care of the tools. Initially, there are two power tools that should be seriously considered.

The first is the power drill. There are many models and types available for purchase and the modeller could well be baffled with choice. It is a serious recommendation that the first power drill to be purchased should be one of both low voltage and variable speed. Dremel and Proxxon drills are both very well made and are useful drills to which attachments can be added for performing alternate jobs. Both are fed with current from a mains input and direct current output transformer, usually packed into a small hard plastic case with the mains power cable and plug already fitted. Some may be run on alternating current, but this is not common.

Although, each drill can be bought as a single unit, it often forms part of a compact boxed set that includes drill bits, abrasive stones, sanding rings and other small parts – all to help the modeller to build his/her models with ease. It is also useful to buy a purpose-made stand to hold the drill firmly and allow it to act as a pedestal drill (as repeated drillings with the drill on a pedestal are much easier to perform than when holding the drill by hand). Because of the low voltage (usually 12 volts) these drills are very safe to use, are light in weight and generally robust.

Although small they can – and will – do virtually all the jobs required of them without problems. In contrast, a mains-powered electric drill is usually large and bulky and is often difficult to use for small holes purely because of its size. Nevertheless, they should not be dismissed out of hand but given consideration, as should all tools.

45

Soldering iron, solder wire, two types of flux and tool holder, this combination would form a good base for soldering work.

The second power tool to consider must really has to be the small belt sander.   With a small belt sander, one can smooth the edges of a cut in almost any material, sand away areas that have been left when sawing and clean parts in preparation for further work or painting. Replacement belts are available in a range of grits and the machine is a wise investment. The sander in the author's workshop is used almost daily and would be sorely missed were it to be removed.

Powered sanding units of the hand held pattern abound and will save the modeller many hours of tedious hard hand sanding. With the many types available and from which to select, it is very much a matter of personal preference. A tug hull made from timber will require a great deal of filling and sanding to gain the fine surface needed for the paint and a powered sander will save a great deal of time.

Moving on, a good soldering iron is a must. Of course, it is possible to use a traditional soldering iron consisting of a pointed piece of copper bolted to a steel rod and fitted with a wooden handle. This would need to be heated in a naked flame to the required temperature and then tinned with solder before being used. However, modern soldering irons are heated by mains electricity, battery or by bottled gas.

The mains electric models are best considered in the first instance, as it is unlikely that the modeller, particularly the beginner, will need to carry out soldering work away from the workshop and its electricity supply. Like so many other tools, soldering irons come in different sizes and vary in power output (heat) according to size. The smallest, at about 12 watts, is suitable only for fine work. Physical size tends to increase with the wattage and 15, 18, 25, 30 and 50 watts are all available. The modeller would be well advised to consider one in the 18-25 watts range for general workshop use. Larger irons can be bought but

Small bench sander – probably the most frequently used unit in the author's workshop.

Pedestal drill, this one is possibly too large for modelling use, smaller units are available and possibly more convenient to use than this one.

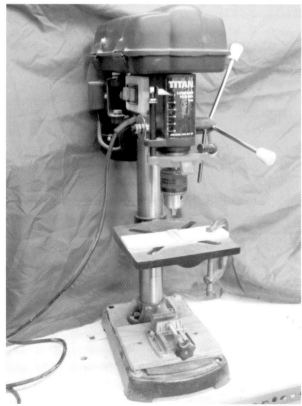

The powered fret saw illustrated is used for the heavier cutting in the author's workshop but is not used frequently and could be considered superfluous.

This Proxxon low voltage drill is a valuable addition to the workshop, it is used almost daily and would be sorely missed if it failed.

only from a specialist tool company and one of 75 to 100 watts is very heavy weight. Large irons of this kind tend to be used for making heavy constructions such as small tanks that need to be used under a degree of pressure.

As with most tools, the modeller will need to learn how to use the soldering iron and how to prepare materials to accept solder so that they can be sealed together. Cleanliness is vital in order to achieve a soundly soldered joint and the buyer should

seek advice and make a number of trial attempts at soldering before applying his/her skills to the model in hand. Solder in wire form is an amalgam of tin and copper with a flux core at the centre. It melts at a specific temperature and will flow easily over a heated, clean surface. There are also some solders that work at higher temperatures, so that joints in the same piece of work can be made without earlier joints melting and falling away. The bookshelves of a good model shop are almost certain to carry some titles on soldering techniques and on brazing, which is a similar method of joining metals.

In the wide range of power saws now available are two that could best be considered by the marine

Looking all of more than twenty years old, the author's workshop needs its annual timber treatment.

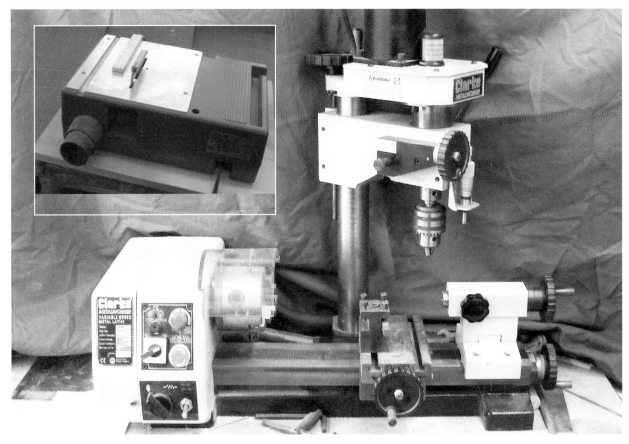

A luxury for most modellers' workshops this lathe and milling unit is used quite often to make master parts in metal for reproduction in casting moulds in addition to producing propellor shafts etc.

(inset) The Proxxon table saw is ideal for cutting planking strips and similar small timber parts, very fine accurate.

modeller. First is the band saw, with either two or three wheels, which is a compact machine carrying a saw blade in the form of a belt. The blade travels at a standard speed and will cut timber up to about three inches in thickness. With care, it will also cut curves, the diameter of which will vary with the width of the blade in use. Overall, it will provide a fairly good edge to the cut material.

Second is the powered fret saw, a much smaller implement that carries a fine blade and can cut round very small corners. Designed initially for the production of jig saw puzzles, a good fretsaw will be an asset. Proxxon, previously mentioned, have two such saws in their range, the smaller of which is very useful for the model ship builder.

The powered pedestal drill has already been mentioned. It will take drill bits that are larger than a small drill held in a stand – although the degree a fairly large pedestal drill will be used is debatable.

Without going into the realms of the machine workshop with lathes and tools designed really for working in metals, the modeller wishing to turn small parts from fine timber or plastics will find that most of the small power drill makers offer accessories (such as lathe attachments) that will allow light turning work to be carried.

One final power-driven tool that can to be considered depends very largely upon the degree of painting that the modeller intends to do. This is the airbrush, with its small compressor and all the essential attachments. Airbrushes of various types can also be fed with air from a pressurised can, but a powered compressor is the preferred choice. In this case, the compressed air can not only be used to power the airbrush but will power a larger spray gun providing a stream of high pressure air that is ideal for blowing away accumulations of dust and swarf. As most compressors will deliver air within which there is a small amount of water, it is advisable always to install a water trap in the pipe system.

As ever, the watchword when buying all types of tools is quality, the very best tools will be expensive but will last the longest and the modeller before investing in an expensive tool would be well advised to seek advice from a fellow modeller who, perhaps, already uses such a tool.

Chapter 9

Building the Model Tug

Having selected the necessary materials, and after collecting drawings and as much data as possible, the modeller may turn to the task of actually building the model.

Initially, we will look at the process of building the model from scratch and then consider kit building and semi-kit building – and go a little further than just the building stage or use of a basic hull, looking in sequence and in detail at additional work.

As used to be the tradition with a full size ship (although not always so today), any model hull has to be built from the keel upwards. If building from scratch, the hull it will be made of wood. Ships were constructed from wood for several millennia, so a similarly built model is in good company and part of an historical lineage.

Fig 9.1: General arrangement drawing of a stan tug.

Ship drawings

A copy of the ships lines drawings are needed if one is to build a ship's hull from scratch. Alas, there is insufficient space within this volume to go into detail about the substantial topic of ship drawings, so it is necessary to cover them only in a summarised form. In essence, a ship's line drawing illustrates the vessel in three ways.

First is what is called the sheer plan – the ship's outline, always of the starboard side, and shown with horizontal lines running from bow to stern at equal intervals. Beneath this is the half-breadth plan, a drawing showing the shape of the hull from centre line and from above known Finally, comes the body plan, usually fitted in a space to one side of the sheer plan or often over it and showing the ship's overall body shape.

All of these drawings are bisected by horizontal

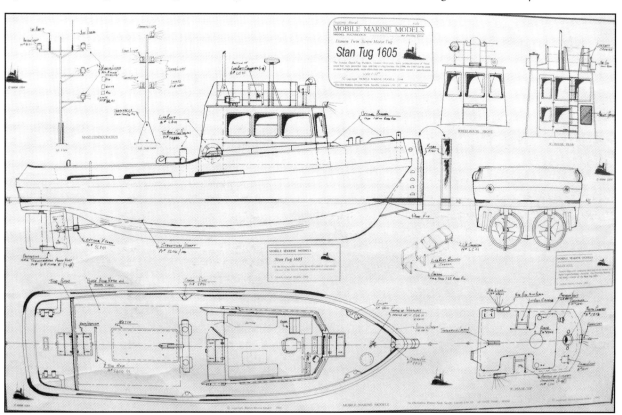

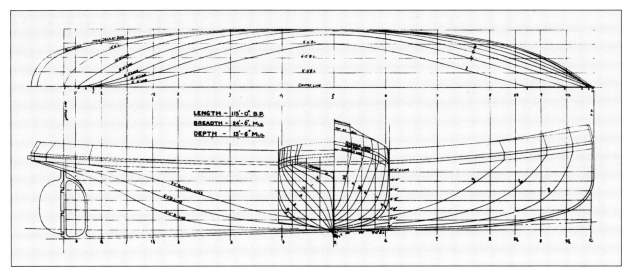

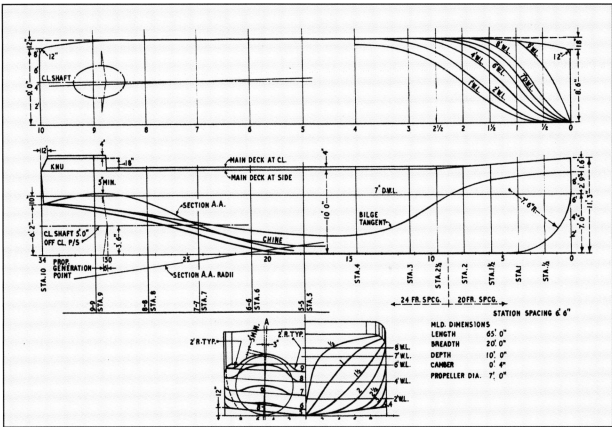

Fig 9.2: Lines drawing for twin screw tug.

Fig 9.3: Lines drawing for vintage steam tug.

hull. This information may seem rather sparse, but study of the drawings here will provide a degree of clarification.

Hull construction

There are basically two ways to build a timber hull. The first is to use a method known as 'bread-and-butter' and the second is called 'plank–on–frame'.

In the writer's experience, the bread-and-butter method – where the timber is the 'bread' and the glue is the 'butter' – is the harder of the two and is also wasteful of timber. Nevertheless, it merits a full explanation.

So, using the horizontal lines of the sheer plan and

and vertical lines. In the case of the sheer plan, the horizontal lines are waterlines and run parallel to the keel, whilst the vertical are stations and run at right angles to the keel. On the half breadth plan, the same horizontal lines and vertical lines are repeated; and then repeated a third time on the body plan. Each individual drawing also carries curved lines that indicate the shape of the ship.

From these drawings, the modeller can determine all the dimensions necessary to build a scale model

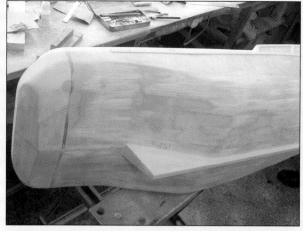

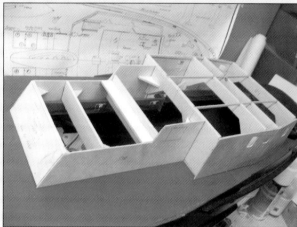

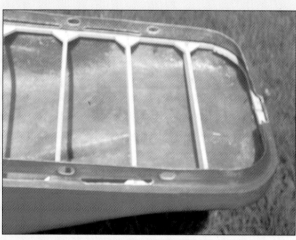

The photographs on this page illustrate stages in building up a timber hull, fitting deck beams and making superstructures.

half-breadth plan, planks of wood are planed to the thickness of the horizontal line spacing. Each plank is then roughly shaped to the outline of its station on the half-breadth plan and, in the case of a working model, the middle is cut away so that it is hollow when the planks are glued together. Then, gluing one plank on top of another, the hull is built up and placed under heavy weights until the glue has fully cured. Next follows the task of planing and sanding the rough shape down to a smooth and accurate hull. Here, carefully cut templates of card or thin ply that match in shape the halves of the body plan can be used to ensure accuracy. Certainly, a fine hull can be built this way, but it is not a task to attempt without a degree of thought.

Alternatively, building a hull by the plank-on-frame method is the easier option – in the author's experience, at least. With this method, the hull is built very much in the same way as a real boat is built in timber. The keel and frames are cut by reference to the profile and body plan drawings, and are then assembled into a skeleton (as shown in the photographs).

This skeleton is then covered in planks of suitable timber, each being glued and pinned to the frames and glued to each other. The planks need to be shaped at either end so that they will form the shape of the bow and stern; or they can terminate close to the bow and stern where blocks of suitable timber can be carved to shape and fitted to complete the unit.

Whilst this all seems to be easy to describe, it is more complicated than the mere description implies. Accurate measurement of each plank is necessary and a fair degree of care is needed to achieve good results. The processes involved have been described in even detail in a number of reference books and in magazine articles (see Appendix 2).

In both the above methods, the completed timber hull will need to receive treatment in order to render it smooth and waterproof as a working model. It will also need various openings cut into it and items such as propeller shafts and rudders have to be made and fitted. Most of this detail is given in later chapters.

The raw hull made by either method will need to be well sanded, using a variety of different grates of abrasive paper. Start this job with a fairly coarse grit (80 or 100) paper and then progress to finer grits until a fine surface is achieved. Achieving a surface suitable for subsequent painting will be easier if the timber is treated with a good grain filler or sanding sealer. When dry, both materials fill the fine parts of the wood grain and allow the sanding to proceed more smoothly. This filling or treatment should be repeated at intervals during the sanding stage. Once the required surface has been achieved, it should be given at least two good coatings of primer and allowed a period of rest before any further work.

For a working model tug, the inside of the hull should be treated with two or three coatings of catalysed resin before prop shafts, etc. are installed. This treatment will render the inside of the hull watertight and will also stiffen the wood fibres so that any water entering the hull will not be absorbed by the timber and thereby prevent any later softening and rot.

Pre-made hulls

The use and treatment of pre-made hulls is obviously much simpler. They are available in two or three forms.

The first and most common pre-made hulls are of moulded in GRP (glass reinforced plastic). They are hard, semi rigid mouldings, usually carrying marked indications as to where propeller shafts and other openings are needed. Depending upon the individual manufacturer, such hulls can be found in different colours, each maker tending to favour one particular another colour scheme. The second type of pre-made hulls are those made in moulded styrene, generally white in colour and usually more flexible than the GRP hulls. Third are the vacuum-formed polystyrene (or similar sheet plastic) hulls.

All three have their place in model ship building, although the stronger GRP hull has to be the favourite for tug building.

Pre-made hulls should first be washed with warm water and a little detergent; then rinsed and allowed to dry naturally. This is necessary, as almost all such hulls will have a small amount of release agent on their surfaces that must be removed in this way in order to allow subsequent coats of paint to adhere fully. Natural drying and avoiding handling with bare hands will also help paint to adhere successfully. Further, all these hulls will need to be stiffened and prepared to accept decks and superstructures, and to allow the installation and necessary removal of the internal 'works'.

Deck beams across the hull and round the perimeter will need to be sited and fixed in place, their location sites being best indicated from the drawings combined with careful consideration and measurement.

The deck beams and other timbers can then be attached and the best adhesive for fixing them to the GRP hull is catalysed resin, the same material from which the hull is made. This can usually be bought in small quantities from motor accessory dealers. When mixed correctly and used as glue, it hardens very quickly via exothermic chemical reaction and so will become too hot to touch as the process proceeds.

Two-part epoxy glue is also suitable – although if the hull is to be immersed in water only use only the slow- curing type; otherwise, the quick drying epoxy cements will soften in water eventually and lose their adhesion.

With styrene hulls, any timber is best secured using epoxy cements after the gluing surface has

Above: Engineroom casing and funnel for a model of Brackengarth. Note that the timber parts have all been filled and sanded to provide a smooth surface before being installed.

Right: Detail of Engineroom casing above

first been roughened; but medium or thick cyano 'Superglue' is also very suitable, although more costly than is the epoxy. Also, because styrene hulls are very flexible, they need very serious stiffening if they are to withstand the rigours of tug towing competitions, etc. There are detailed descriptions of hull building within the author's other books Scale Model Tugs & Trawlers and Working Scale Model Merchant Ships (see Appendix 2).

Semi-kits

As mentioned before, some makers of model ship kits offer their products in small packages – generally called 'semi-kits' – that enable the modeller to spread the possible high cost over the building period. Such 'semi-kits' do not include finished or pre-drawn parts for decks or pre-cut timbers, etc., but do include sheet material and (often) a set of line-drawn templates to aid the modeller. Normally, there are usually no written instructions as such, but the kits do provide the builder with a relatively wide field of working,

as the materials can be modified easily to produce a similar but different model to that depicted on the package.

However, a word of warning in respect of the semi-kit; such kits are rarely suitable for the complete beginner. A degree of experience gained from making a previous model ship – probably a small one – is necessary before attempting a semi-kit.

Decks and superstructures

The decks of the tug model are the next parts to be fitted. The various methods of fixing the decks to

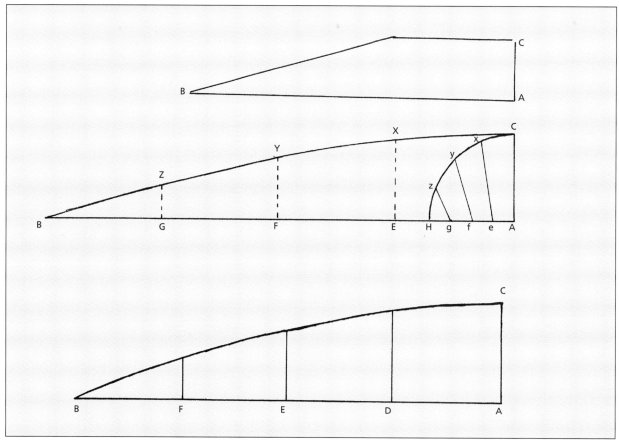

the hull vary only slightly and any differences are mainly a result of the material in use both for the deck and the hull. In most cases, the majority of decks for model tugs will be found to be made from fine, marine quality plywood; but decks of styrene or GRP can also be made. Whether the hull is made of timber or of GRP, or even of moulded ABS (acrylonitrile butadiene styrene), the line of the main deck must be clearly defined and marked upon the hull. If the hull is of timber, the deck line is usually the top edge of the hull. This position of the deck needs to be measured carefully and, at the very least, marked at each frame station and vertically from the keel. The hull will need to be sanded to this line – and if the deck is to lie on top of the hull, then the deck line

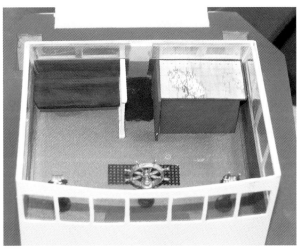

Opposite: Finished model of *Ayton Cross* on the water

Right above: Wheelhouse interior showing wheel and telegraphs etc

Right: Wheelhouse interior showing chart table etc.

Opposite below Fig 9.4: Deck camber calculation charts

Below: Beautifully detailed interior of the wheelhouse of a model tug – *photo courtesy of Model Slipway*

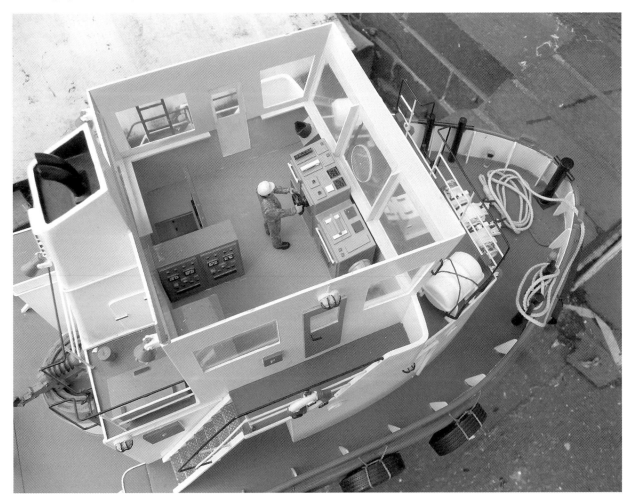

Left: Superstructure and detail of 'BRACKENGARTH'

Below Left: Superstructure of model Brackengarth to show finish and detail.

Right: Wheelhouse of Brackengarth showing illuminated navigation lamps, fire monitors etc.

Below: Further detail of wheelhouse above.

should be drawn and the hull cut down to allow for the thickness of the deck material. If the deck is to lie inside the hull, then small supporting blocks of timber must be glued between the frames in order to support the deck edge.

With GRP and ABS hulls, the deck edges need to be marked inside the hull itself. Most pre-formed hulls incorporate the bulwarks, so that the decks will be below the top edge of the hull by the height of the bulwarks. In such examples, any perimeter supports for the hull must allow not only for the depth of the bulwarks, but also for the thickness of the finished deck. Deck- edge supports can be made from a square section timber strip of 6-10 mm section that is secured to the GRP sides by an appropriate adhesive. The best, in this case, is catalysed polyester resin, as this is the material of which the hull is made; but two-part epoxy resins will also suffice.

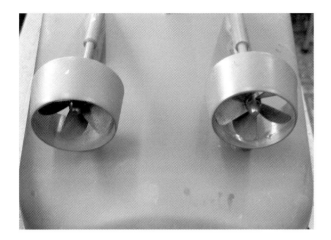

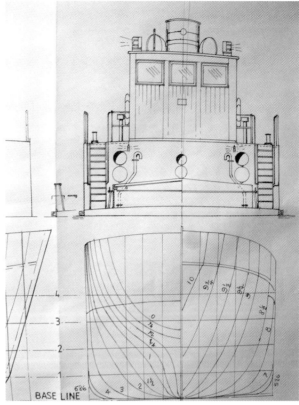

Twin fixed Kort nozzles and propellers on stern of model tug under construction.

Left above: Close detail of bow deck of tug to show windlass, barred anchor cable, hatches, ventilators etc.

Left below: Stern deck of tug showing tow bows, capstan, tow hook and grating over rudder access.

Right: Drawing showing section of lines of a model tug and the wheelhouse.

Fitting timber strip like these takes time and care, as they need to curve to the sheer of the hull and to the curves at bow and stern. In order to ease strips around the tight curves at bow and stern, make small saw cuts in the timber about halfway through the width. Such cuts will permit it to bend more freely. In addition, the adhesive should not be allowed to run on to the top face of the timber strips.

On some tugs, the sheer of the curve of the deck from bow to stern can be pronounced, whilst on others, it is almost a straight line. Camber is term used to describe the curve across the deck from one side to the other. On all but the very latest tugs, this is a curve that is highest in the centre and lowest at the deck edges. It is arranged in this way so as to shed water quickly and easily. However, most of the very latest tugs have a straight-line camber or none at all; but straight line is, as for the curved type, remains high in the centre and sloping to the sides. To ensure accuracy when installing decks and deck beams, both decks and beams should be marked with a fore and aft centre line. Calculating the camber curve is shown in Fig. 9/4, and deck beams to support the decks at various intervals should all have the camber cut on their top edge.

Deck beams are needed at prescribed intervals and will have to be attached to the perimeter timber deck supports, where possible the beams will benefit from additional security of small triangular pieces of scrap plywood being glued between beam and edge timber as illustrated. Before any beams are fitted or measured for fitting, the question of access to the interior of the hull for fitting drive equipment, radio, etc. should be

addressed. Sensibly, the largest access will generally be through the removal of the detachable superstructure – so that any deck beams in way of this will have to be cut away. Other access points may be required, and these too will interfere with the location of the deck beams. The skilful modeller will take note of this and arrange the deck beams accordingly.

The decks can next be cut to shape and prepared for fitting. It is wise to make cardboard templates of the proposed decks and to use these in order to ensure that the final deck, of ply or other material, will fit without problem. It is much easier to cut card and make mistakes at that stage than to cut expensive timbers and similar material. Cereal packets are an excellent source of reasonable card stock.

Decks of marine quality plywood are the best for fitting to the timber hull, although other materials can be used. Decks for the GRP and plastic hulls can often best be made from 2.0-mm thick styrene, but gluing styrene to timber will need either 'Superglue' or two-part epoxy for truly secure joints. Furthermore, where the deck has to be planked to follow the decks of the prototype, then strips of thin timber will be easier to glue to a ply deck than to one of styrene. However, the choice of deck material is in the hands of the modeller where scratch building is concerned - although building from a kit or semi-kit then usually involves deck material supplied by the kit maker.

Coamings will be needed around all access holes in the deck, once it has been installed, They are required in order that any superstructure, etc. sits safely over the access hole and remains in place under most working conditions. These coamings will also prevent deck water from entering the hull and causing damage to delicate electronics and other equipment. They are easily made from strips of plywood 2.0 or 3.0-mm thick (that is, some 0.08 to 0.12 inches) and that are glued to the deck aperture edges, reinforced where necessary by small scraps of ply or strip timber. The photographs of coamings show how they are installed.

Deck planks

Many tugs have decks made from timber overlaying the steel structure beneath. Such deck planking is laid to precise rules that laid down by the official ship Classification Societies (e.g. Lloyds Register, American Bureau of Shipping, Bureau Veritas, Germanischer Lloyd, etc.). However, not all tugs have all of their decks made of timber, with some having timber only in only specified places and others using timber only over accommodation areas, etc. A deck will often be covered in timber planks in areas where most work is done, the planks being laid in such a way as to allow easy replacement in the event of the timber wearing down.

Where the deck is planked, it is usual for a 'king plank' to run centrally along the deck, from bow to stern. This plank will be slightly wider than the other planks and will, of course, be laid where the deck camber is highest. Deck planks on a full-size tug used to be of teak, a very expensive timber. Consequently, these days, they are usually of deal, each plank being 75 mm (about 3 inches) thick and 125 mm (about 5 inches) wide as a general rule. They can be simulated on a model with strips of lime or of thin birch plywood, a rule of thumb being to make such planks of the chosen material of strips 1.0 mm (only about 0.04 inch) thick and of the width indicated by the scale of the model. For example, if the model were built at just under 0.5 or 1/2 inch (10 mm) to the foot, then the deck planks would be approximately 4.0 mm (0.16 inches) wide.

All real deck planking was (and often still is) caulked. Traditionally, this was usually with oakum and pitch, oakum being the teased out strands of rope, which was driven into the small space between each plank and over which is poured hot pitch. Today, although the method is similar, pitch is replaced by a synthetic material that can be poured cold. Special tools called caulking irons are used to drive the teased rope fibres in between the planks. This can be depicted on a model in three ways.

The first and easiest method of showing the caulking is to draw a black, fibre marking pen along the edge of the timber plank before it is laid. The second is to glue thin black card to the edge of the plank; and the third is to use black cord laid and glued between the planks as they are glued in place.

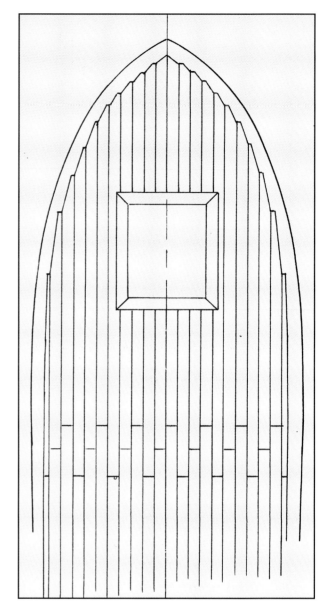

Fig 9.5: Typical deck planking arrangement.

All three methods have their adherents and the author, who favours the first, has tried them all.

The rule regarding the lay of the planks is that no butt joints may coincide on the same beam closer than three planks apart. This means that a butt joint between the ends of two planks may not occur in the same line across the deck closer than three planks apart.

The material from which decks are planked comes in random lengths. These that can be as short as 5 m (around 15 feet) up to as long as nearly 8 m (25 feet) and the shipwright attending to laying the deck will arrange his butt joints according to the available lengths of plank to avoid waste wherever possible. The photographs here illustrate some typical decks.

Electric Drives and Batteries

Chapter 10

Having made and completed the hull, the working model will need to be outfitted with its drive equipment. This is best tackled before any decks are laid, so that access is easy. However, the drive gear must also be installed where it will be accessible after the decks are sealed down. As a result, the modeller must consider where motors can best be placed, beneath hatches or deckhouses, for easy access.

Sensibly, the first pieces of drive equipment to be installed will be the propeller shaft(s). Apart from the timber-built version, shaft locations are usually marked upon the hull. The selected shaft – of a length to suit the location of the motor(s) and couplings – should be fitted carefully. The hull will need to have a slot through which the shaft can emerge.

Next, the shaft will need to be securely sealed to the hull, using either catalysed resin or a similar body filler. It will need to rise within the hull to a small degree, in order to permit the motor on its mounting and with the appropriate coupling to be sensibly positioned. Most model ship shops carry a range of suitable units (couplings) to connect motor to propeller shaft. Again care is needed to instal these carefully. The run of the motor shaft, its coupling and propeller shaft need to be almost exactly in line in order to allow efficient and strain-free running. If the running of units cannot be maintained exactly in line, then a so-dubbed double coupling must be used in order to keep the transmission system resistance as low as possible. There are NO alternatives to this rule.

Any tug (model or full-size) needs to have the attributes of a high bollard pull that is matched to a sensible power input. In more technical terms, this is expressed as high torque and low fuel consumption.

In a model context, this means a good, strong motor that draws upon low amperage. A high-amperage motor will drain batteries quite rapidly and deliver only a short duration of running.

Until comparatively recent times, the author would have invariably recommended a fairly high-speed, low-current consuming motor – driving the propeller

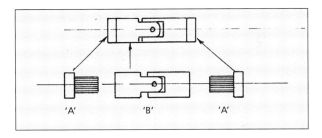

Fig 10.2: Single propellor shaft coupling by Huco – others available

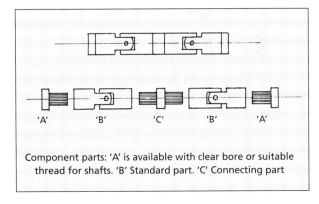

Component parts: 'A' is available with clear bore or suitable thread for shafts. 'B' Standard part. 'C' Connecting part

Fig 10.2: Double propellor shaft coupling by Huco

Fig 10.1: Typical propeller shaft as available commercially

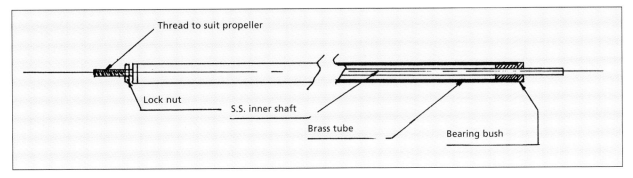

Thread to suit propeller

Lock nut

S.S. inner shaft

Brass tube

Bearing bush

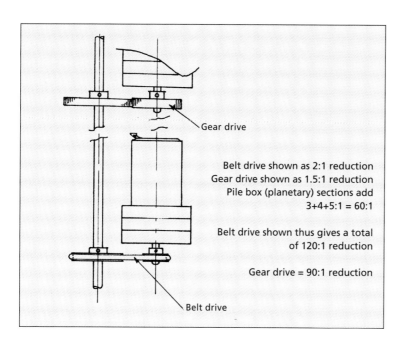

Fig 10.5: Motor and planetary gearbox drive to side paddles

Belt drive shown as 2:1 reduction
Gear drive shown as 1.5:1 reduction
Pile box (planetary) sections add
3+4+5:1 = 60:1

Belt drive shown thus gives a total
of 120:1 reduction

Gear drive = 90:1 reduction

Fig 10.4: Worm and wheel drive for paddle

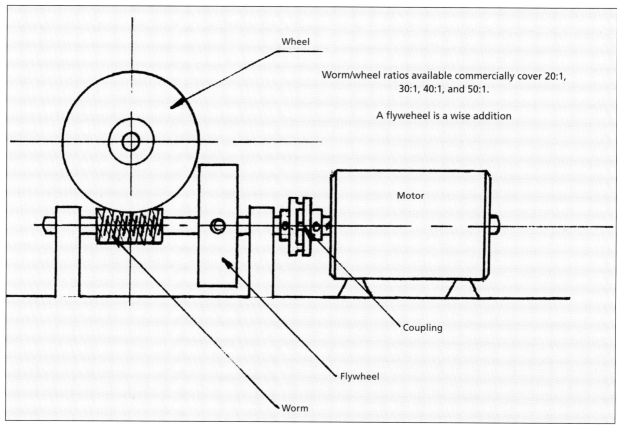

Worm/wheel ratios available commercially cover 20:1,
30:1, 40:1, and 50:1.

A flyweheel is a wise addition

shaft through a reduction gearbox. (In fact, this is exactly how a full size tug is generally driven.) Whilst this is still a very wise course to adopt, there are now available from most good model motor suppliers a range of multi-pole, slow-running electric motors that have very low current consumption, but with high torque. Of course, they are expensive; but not unduly so and are thus worthy of consideration.

The hoary question that always arises is: what motor do I fit? The simple answer is just as often: "how long is a piece of string?" In other words, there are (quite literally) hundreds of small electric motors on the market and a great many of them are suitable for driving a model tug. It is impossible to test them all; and so the best advice one can give is to seek help from a more experienced modeller – or to consult the maker if constructing a kit-built model. Most model shop staff are capable of giving good advice, particularly if they are also members of a model boat club and sail their own models.

As a general guide, a first step is to seek advice upon which motor to fit to one's selected model. Secondly, ascertain the maximum current upon which the motor will draw under load. Also, if possible, check out the current (in amps) that is drawn at the moment the motor is stalled, i.e. when it is stopped deliberately by gripping the running shaft.

The running current compared to the rating of the batteries will give an indication of how long the model will run on one charge of the battery system. Batteries are rated in voltage and ampere/hours, i.e. 12 volts x 10 amp/hours – which means simply that if you draw 1 amp/ hour from the fully-charged battery, it will last (or close to) 10 hours. If the motor then draws, say, 2 amp/per hour, then the battery will last only 5 hours. From these sorts of figures, one can determine what to fit and which battery to use.

Sealed lead-acid batteries are the usual means of providing power for the model tug. They are fairly compact but heavy and so readily form part of the ballast needed to bring the model down to its waterline.

It is also important that the tug, full size or model, has its propeller(s) well below the water for maximum power.

Quite often, the geared motor will be easier to instal within the small hull, where space can be a problem. It is a proven fact that a motor drawing 6 amps, and driving directly a 50-mm (2-inch) diameter propeller, will draw only 1.5 amps when driving the same propeller through a 2:1 reduction gear – and with little or no difference in performance. Thus, any modeller can see that there are a host of alternatives by way of driving the model tug by electric motor and batteries. It is no cliché that the old principle remains: buy the best that you can afford. The better motors are those made by the manufacturers whose products have stood the test of time.

Installing the chosen electric motor also needs consideration. Some modellers will bed their motors on a silicon compound and hold them in place with rubber bands. This is NOT good practice. The motor should be fixed firmly in a sensibly made mounting and aligned with the propeller shaft, with it's coupling as nearly 'true' as is possible. Variations in the alignment of motor and shaft should be kept within the closest limits attainable; and double couplings should be used when necessary.

In addition, the whole drive system should be designed and built to be as friction-free as possible. That the motor(s) need to be secure is also a 'must'. It is quite possible that a loosely installed motor will be dislodged if the propeller is caught in weed. Indeed, in such unfortunate circumstances it can actually be thrown clean through the deck of the model – causing damage not only to the model, but also to surrounding area. Admittedly such an occurrence is more likely to happen when using a high-speed motor than with a slower running unit; but it is always a possibility and thus should be avoided.

The photographs illustrate applications of electric motors in a range of model ships and tugs. The single-screw drive is obviously the simplest and easiest to install, whereas the twin-screw drive is open to more variation; and the multi-screw installation even more complex.

The depth of the model hull and the beam, complicated by any 'rise of floor', restricts the space available for drive motor(s). In addition, the size of the chosen drive motor also affects its place within the hull, along with access to the motor(s) through the deck adds more complications. As a result, the modeller must select all drive equipment within these parameters.

Whilst a large and slow-running, high-torque motor would be the ideal choice, there is little point in buying it if it will not fit into the hull of the model. Always study the drawings of the ship very carefully. Obtain an accurate, full-size scale drawing of the model; or have the drawings that provided with the kit suitably enlarged or reduced to the correct scale.

Slow speed high torque Buehler electric motor.
Photo courtesy of Model Motors Direct

Similar but larger electric motor.
Photo courtesy of Model Motors Direct

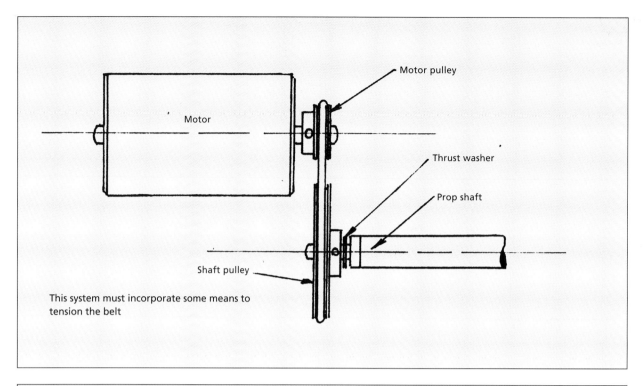

Motor pulley

Thrust washer

Prop shaft

Motor

Shaft pulley

This system must incorporate some means to tension the belt

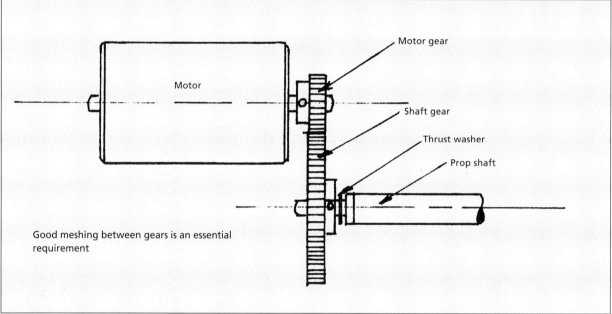

Motor gear

Shaft gear

Thrust washer

Prop shaft

Motor

Good meshing between gears is an essential requirement

Use these drawings to lay out the proposed motor(s) shafts and couplings by laying the actual units on the drawing in the proposed location. Then work from there.

Measure and mark such locations carefully within the hull, so that errors will not occur; and remember to measure twice and mark or cut once.

It is possible to mount twin motors side-by-side in a suitable mounting – so that they lie parallel to each other and allow the respective couplings to connect with the twin propeller shafts accurately and create a neat installation. This method of mounting twin motors also allows the subsequent wiring to be run neatly and be set away from cables carrying radio signals. A number of methods of mounting drive

Top Fig 10.6: Typical belt reduction arrangement

Above Fig 10.7: Simple gear reduction arrangement

Above opposite top Fig 10.8: Double reduction gear system

Right Fig 10.9: Diagrammatic arrangement for Azimuthing thruster

Right: Twin motors installed in a small model tug illustrating double couplings and servo for rudder control.

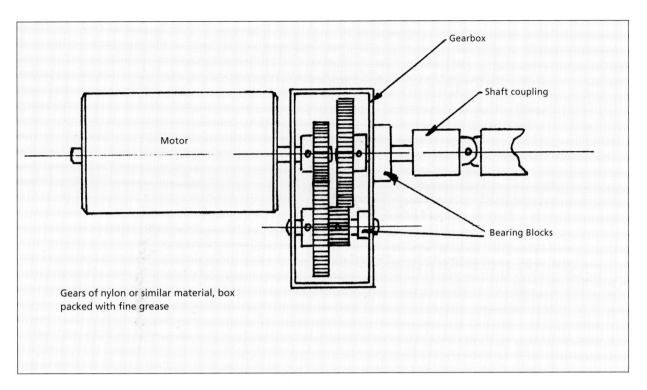

Gears of nylon or similar material, box packed with fine grease

motors securely are illustrated in the accompanying diagrams and photographs.

The model tug kit making specialists Mobile Marine Models (see Appendix 2) recommend motors of high torque. They carry an excellent range of such motors, are ideal for the large-scale tug (1:32 and 1:24), but are usually too large and heavy for the tug built to smaller scales. In such cases, the modeller needs to seek out smaller units.

Overall, in order to gain increased power with low consumption, there is no alternative than to fit a reduction gearbox between the motor and shaft.

A number of suppliers offer motors with gearboxes

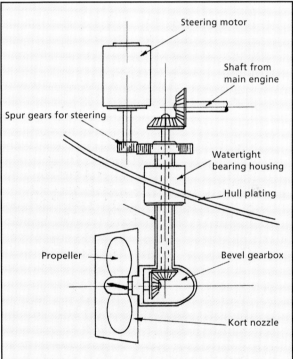

that are permanently attached and providing given reduction ratios. Possibly the best known of these is the Marx Luder range of motors, known as 'Monoperm', 'Decaperm' and 'Hectaperm'.

These motors have been in production for some years. The Monoperm can be bought as solely a motor, or complete with a 'pile' gearbox. The Decaperm is supplied as already fitted with a 2.5:1 reduction gearbox at one end and a straight shaft at the other. Hectaperm, the largest of the trio, can also be supplied with either type of pattern gearbox fully installed.

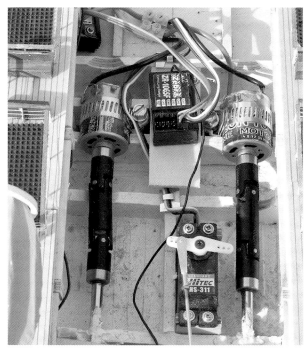

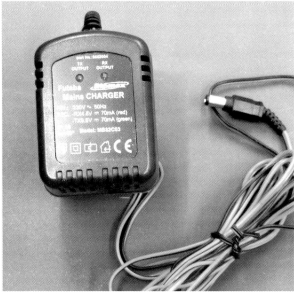

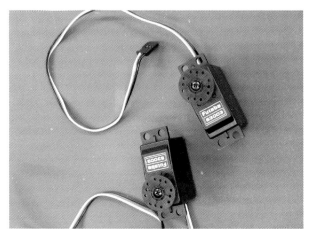

Top Left Linkage connecting twin rudders to servo unit

Top right Detail of twin motors and servo to also show cable clips

Above left: Mains charger for use with Futaba Skysport Radio outfit

Above Twin servo and switch harness as supplied with Futaba Skysport outfit

Right top: Further pictures of twin motor installation including radio receiver and speed control units

Right: Twin motors and battery tray in *Ayton Cross*

Far Right: Additional battery tray in *Ayon Cross*

Bottom Right: View of motor installation in *Ayon Cross* looking from the *bow.*

The pile gearbox is a unit in four sections, each section containing planetary gears that combine to give a specific speed reduction. Section one will provide 3:1, section two will give 4:1, section three will give 5:1, and the last section will give 6:1.

The combined reduction of all four sections in service will give an overall reduction of 360:1. This means the motor running at 3600 revolutions per minute has its output shaft running at only ten. Each section can be detached from the motor so that the modeller can gain the reduction in speed he or she needs. As previously stated, the suggested propeller speed for a scale model tug in the range of 1:50 up to 1:25 is in the order of 1000-1200 r.p.m in free air. Faster speeds for marine propellers are unnecessary; they waste fuel and will not improve the speed of the model. So, unless it is designed for high-speed use, high speed is best avoided.

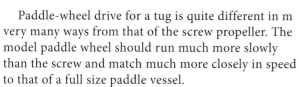

Paddle-wheel drive for a tug is quite different in m very many ways from that of the screw propeller. The model paddle wheel should run much more slowly than the screw and match much more closely in speed to that of a full size paddle vessel.

For example, a suggested speed for the Graupner paddle wheel set would be a full speed of 100-150 r.p.m. Of course, the drive will be athwartships and, therefore, a geared- or belt-drive will be the best possible option.

It is possible to site the drive motor parallel to

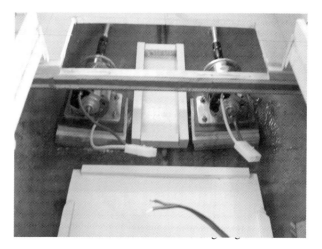

can be recommended. The motor size for a paddle set is again debatable and possible testing. However, the author has driven a 1-m (48-inch) long paddle vessel weighing in at some 12 kg (around 27 lb) using a Monoperm super motor driving through a 25:1 one worm and wheel, showing clearly that it is possible to use quite small motors with suitable gearing.

Drive batteries

As mentioned already, the recommended battery for the working model tug must be the sealed lead-acid unit. Although quite weighty, such batteries come in a range of sizes and are available from a number

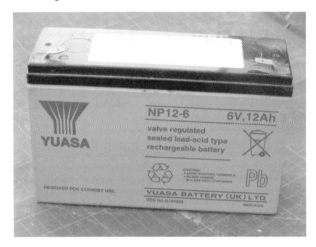

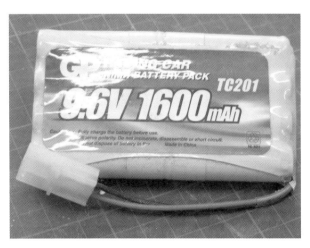

Left top: Typicla 6 volt/12 ampere hour sealed lead acid battery – ideal for supplying current to model tug motor(s) and for provideing some degree of balast.

Left centre: Pen cells (AA type) frequently used for powering radio transmitters and receivers

Left bottom: 9 volt 1600 mAh rechargeable nickel metal hydride battery. pack. Suitable for drive motor power or similar use.

Above: Simple and cheap unit for testing battery capacity, ideal for checking on the condition of rechargeable batteries of most kinds.

of stores and mail order outlets. Provided they are charged correctly and kept in a clean condition, they will prove to be long lasting. However, they need to be charged using only with their specified, correct charging unit. Using a car's battery charger will cause damage; and using a charger designed for rechargeable Ni-CD (nickel-cadmium) or Ni-mh (nickel-metal hydride) batteries is also unworkable. In any case, a charger for the sealed type of lead-acid battery of model size is not expensive and is a worthwhile investment.

It is also possible to drive the motor(s) of the model tug using rechargeable batteries such as Ni-Cd. They come in packs to give selected voltages and selected amperage, as well as being light in weight and easy to instal. The latest type of battery along similar lines are known as Li-ion (lithium-ion) and have extensive current capacities and none of the so-termed 'charging memory' that is the failing of Ni-Cd batteries. All types of these dry batteries (as opposed to the 'wet' lead-acid type) are, in general, expensive and usually obtainable best from the specialist supplier (see Appendix 2).

Chargers for such units vary tremendously both in type and in price. Some will charge a battery set overnight or in a similar space of time, whilst others will recharge in a matter of an hour or so. Some function by first discharging the battery pack completely before recharging and most will switch automatically to trickle charge conditions once the pack is back up to full capacity. The specialist supplier of batteries and battery packs is in the unique position of providing the model tug master with expert advice on these matters.

Installing the selected battery within the model hull also calls for some attention. The battery or batteries will be usually reasonable heavy – especially if lead-acid – and they must be fitted securely to prevent them from moving when the model will in the water. A loose battery can easily shift inside the hull and cause the model to capsize.

Another side benefit is that the majority of batteries in model tugs form a part of the ballast needed to stabilise the model. But like ballast of any kind, must be fixed firmly to prevent movement of any kind. A sealed lead-acid battery should therefore have a substantial frame in which it can sit securely, but from which it can also be removed easily if necessary. It should be located so as to aid the balance of the model and be set low in the hull – and in a place where the tug master can reach the connections for cleaning, etc. – that is, be as accessible as the drive motor(s). As a tug generally has a fairly large superstructure, making it detachable will aid access to the inside of the hull.

Propellers

Little has been said about propellers or paddles for driving the model tug. It is quite possible for the model tug master to make propeller(s) from brass sheet and tube. However, such a task requires a degree of experience and often a great deal of time ensuring that the unit runs fully balanced. Consequently, the vast majority of model tug makers will seek to buy these parts from the specialist supplier – where propellers come in a number of forms and with blades numbering from two to more than seven, according to the tug's duty. The better quality units are of brass or bronze and are made to very precise measurements.

The propeller needed to run within a Kort nozzle has its blades shaped to run closely within the circle of the nozzle in order to provide maximum thrust. One model tug specialist has a very high quality range of Kort nozzles that are cast in hard plastic. These are matched by propellers produced by an equally qualified specialist propeller maker so as to make matched sets (see Appendix 2).

Ready-made paddle outfits are rare, and only one company (Graupner) produces a complete paddle unit in kit form and in hard plastic. The paddle tug modeller whose scale of model differs from that of the Graupner paddle set must make the paddles from scratch. From one of the diagrams (pages 13 and 14), it will be noted that fully feathering paddles are fairly complex. Nevertheless, they should not be beyond the capabilities of the modeller who can carry out good quality soldering and who can handle sheet and strip brass or similar material.

A simple, non-feathering paddle is relatively easy to make from styrene sheet, strip and tube, and such a unit will work reasonably well – although not as efficiently as will a feathering paddle set. Paddle tugs were invariably able to run their paddles independently and thereby provide a high degree of manoeuvrability. The model paddle tug can also be driven in a similar way if twin electric motors are used – but it is not to be recommended. Contra-rotating paddles will very easily cause a small model to capsize, as one paddle digging deep into the water and the other climbing out of it is a recipe for disaster. Therefore, author would advise strongly that all model paddle driven ships have their paddles driven from a single paddle shaft.

So far, information has dealt with the conventional method of driving the tug through shaft(s) and propeller(s). However, many tugs are driven by alternative means, such as the Schottel unit, the azimuthing unit and the Voith Schneider drive. In the context of modelling, all of these systems are designed for electric motor drive – whereas in modern, full-sized tugs they are driven by compression-ignition (diesel) engines or by an electric motor with power created by diesel-driven generators.

The Schottel drive is available currently in two sizes, both from Graupner (see Appendix 2). Both are arranged for drive by electric motor and have inbuilt Kort nozzles. The smaller of the two units is the less efficient and has both servo motor and drive motor separately mounted within the hull of the model. The larger and more efficient unit has the servo mounting built in and needs only the main drive motor to be separately mounted. Both units provide not only propulsion, but also steering and are, in effect, inboard/outboard drive units.

Units like these that are installed in full size tugs provide a degree of manoeuvrability greater than does a conventional propeller and shaft drive. They are not difficult to instal in a model, but the modeller should

Azimuth thruster on a tug in dry dock.

Azimuth thruster showing anti-corrosion anodes attached to nozzle.

Close detail of full size Azimuth thruster.

be aware that they need a fair degree of space beneath the deck and one that is much greater than for the conventional drive. The height between the bottom of the hull and the deck at the stern of most tugs is restrictive and, therefore, the modeller should be sure that adequate space is available for the drive units described.

Schottel drive units allow the propeller/Kort nozzle sections to swivel through 120 to 180 degrees for steering the ship – and this is arranged through built-in gearing from a standard servo motor drive. The larger of the two units has the added facility of being supplied with two propellers, one for left hand drive and one for right hand drive, allowing the modeller to select the rotation desired.

In the case of twin-screw drive, one can be fitted to run clockwise and the other anti-clockwise, with the propellers simply fitted and exchanged as required.

Azimuthing propulsion units are virtually identical to Schottel drive, except that they can be revolved through 360 degrees giving drive in all directions. There are no commercially made azimuthing units available at the time of writing but no doubt the enterprising tug modeller will come up with a means of adapting the currently available units. The azimuthing drive is popular with some types of tug and in the case of the modeller wishing to use the Schottel units but needs similar manoeuvrability then the addition of athwartships thrusters at bow and near the stern will probably give similar results.

The Voith Schneider propulsion (VPS) system is very different and is fitted to many modern tugs in full size. It comprises a series of vertical blades set in rotating rings suspended beneath the ship and driven from a suitable diesel engine. By varying the angle of the blades, the unit will drive the ship in different directions, control of the blade angles being carried out through a system of levers. This system is quite complex in construction but is very efficient in full size practice. Its use allows the tug, or similar, vessels to manoeuvre quickly and easily, even in quite small areas.

Each VPS unit is tailored to suit the specific vessel in which it is to be installed, and takes into account the particular tasks of the ship. Although the manufacturers make standard units, consultation with the makers by the ship builders is essential to ensure correct and efficient operation.

VPS units are particularly complex for the modeller to make, although, with good workshop facilities, they can be successfully built. Graupner produce a fully working VPS drive unit in model form but only to a single scale size (as illustrated in Fig 10.9). The book Voith Schneider-Antreib im Selbstbau by Bossart and Schultz carries very clear and detailed instructions for installation; and its photographs illustrate twin belt-driven units that are driven from vertically mounted motors (as it is possible to mount the drive motors horizontally and to provide the primary drive via gears).

A further point relative to azimuthing and VPS drives is that they are often placed on the full size tug in unconventional positions. Many, for example, are fitted quite well forward and, in effect, pull the tug forward rather than pushing it. Often, two drive units will also be mounted, one ahead of the other or side-by-side, in a forward position. Fitting these units in a position forward of amidships puts the units below the superstructure – and, of course, means that there will then be ample head room within the hull to install such sizable drives.

Chapter 11

Steam Engines and Boilers

The early development of the tug and the steam engine has been dealt with in previous chapters. Here, we look at outfitting the model steam tug with a working model steam engine and suitable boiler. Until comparatively recent times, there were a number of manufacturers making small steam outfits ideal for installation in the model tug. Some have ceased to produce such machinery, leaving only a few specialist makers still in business. By virtue of their complexity and need for a very fine degree of accuracy, the model steam outfit is a costly unit to produce commercially. Those that are available are described and shown in this chapter.

However, it is also possible for the modeller with some experience to build their own steam plant from the basic raw materials. As a halfway option, some machine tool and model shops also offer kits of castings and material from which the competent modeller can assemble a small engine and build a boiler.

In general, the engines usually used for small models are of two alternative patterns. The first is the engine with oscillating cylinders and the second is the engine with slide valves. The former is the simplest of all steam engines and, in full size, was the one preferred for paddle driven ships in the early steam years. Its cylinders oscillate over a burnished plate that is drilled in selected places, so that the steam enters and pushes down the piston. As the piston moves, the steam exhaust port is opened and the used steam evacuated, the oscillations being caused by the piston rod revolving round the heavy flywheel and moving the cylinder from side to side.

In the slide valve engine, the steam is fed to the cylinders and pistons through a steam chest, within which a slide is driven, that it opens inlet and outlet ports as the engine shaft revolves. This engine is more

Fig 11.1 : Simple cylindrial boiler

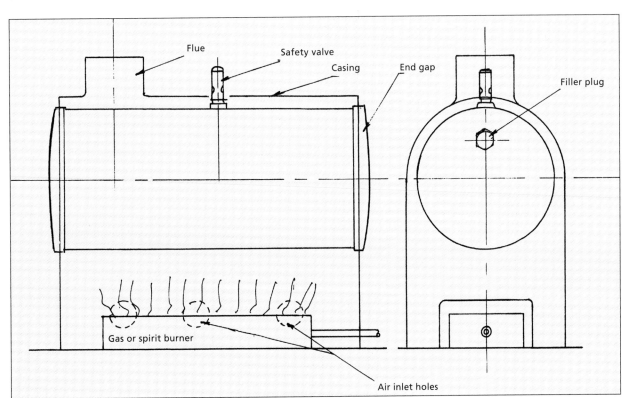

Flue
Safety valve
Casing
End gap
Filler plug
Gas or spirit burner
Air inlet holes

Above, right and below: Differing views of a twin-cylinder steam driven paddle engine, about ten years old, by Marten Howes and Bayliss.

efficient, having fewer places from which steam might leak and ensuring that the quantity of steam fed to the pistons is very much more accurately controlled by the slide valves.

Both engines are reversible. For marine duty, the twin cylinder version was preferred to single

cylinder units, as some of the latter were not self-starting. Like their original counterparts, model versions of both engines need to be lubricated using oil made specifically for use with steam plants – the usual method of providing lubrication to the engine being what is called a displacement lubricator. Quite simply, a displacement lubricator is a cylinder with a removable cover at the top and a small drain with valve at the bottom. Through the top of the cylinder runs a small-bore tube through which the main steam supply to the engine is fed. On the underside of this tube, where it runs through the cylinder, is bored a small hole. The cylinder is filled with oil and a small drop of water is first added. Then, as the engine draws steam through the tube from the boiler, it also carries water vapour along. This vapour condenses as a water drop in the lubricator cylinder, causing the oil level to rise where it is collected by the flow of steam and fed into the working parts of the engine. It is very simple, and very effective.

The model boiler needed to supply steam to the

Fig 11.2 : Simple horizontal boiler

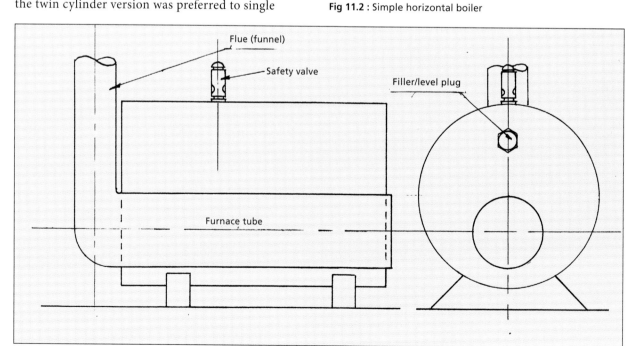

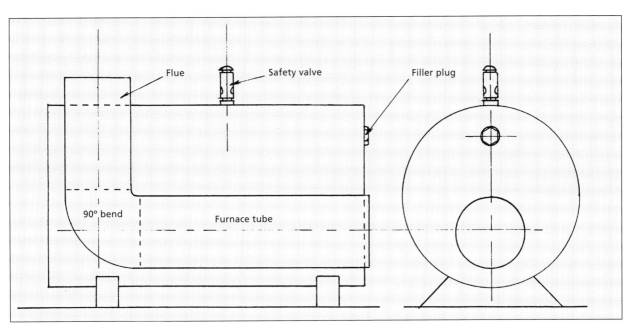

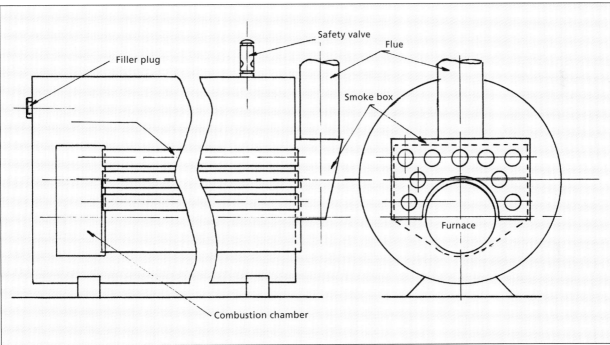

Top Fig 11.3 : Horizontal boiler with internal flue

Above Fig 11.4 : Horizontal return tube boiler
with single furnace

selected engine(s) is usually supplied with the steam
engine as a complete plant. However, just as it is
possible for a competent modeller to build a steam
engine, so it is possible to build a steam boiler. Some
makers offer boilers and engines as separate units and
the modeller can thus build a steam outfit specifically
to suit a ship of choice.

The most common boilers used for the model ship
are the vertical, cross-tube pattern and the horizontal
internal flue pattern. Each has its use and both are
illustrated here. There are two other types (Figs 11/5
& 11/6) and the three drum pattern which is the most
complicated pattern but possibly the most efficient
shown in Fig. 11/7.

Firing a small steam boiler is most often achieved
using LPG (liquefied petroleum gas) obtained in
pressurised cans and burned within the furnace
or flue of the boiler, using a specific pattern of gas
burner. It is possible to fire some boilers using
methylated spirit or even a pressurised paraffin or
petrol burner, although the latter can be difficult to
control and thus can be dangerous. These methods of
raising steam are discussed later.

The oscillating steam engine
The oscillating steam engine is shown in the
accompanying diagrams and photographs. It is very
simple in operation and very effective when sized

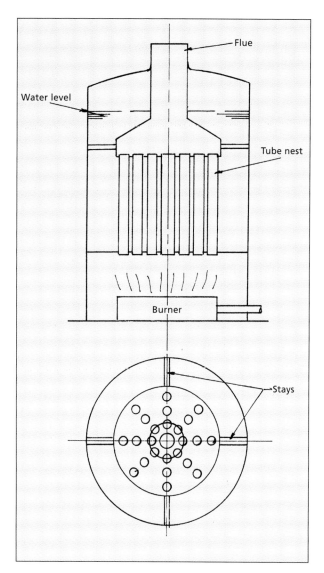

to suit a model. It is easily reversed and controlled – from slow to high speed – through a single lever. However, if not assembled correctly and accurately, it can be wasteful of steam

In single-cylinder form (Fig. 11/8), it is not usually self-starting, thus the twin-cylinder engine is to be recommended (Fig. 11/9). As previously stated, the oscillating steam plant was first used in paddle steamers right up into the 1950s, although some of the latest paddle vessels were driven by triple expansion steam engines.

For models of the size generally seen on the local lake, a twin-cylinder engine with both cylinders of equal size is the most common. A compound steam engine, where the steam is first fed to a high-pressure cylinder and then to a second, larger and low-pressure cylinder, is very rare. Such engines need to be fairly large in order to gain substantially from the more economical use of steam. A model compound engine is shown in one of the photographs [11-01 and 11-02 hereabouts if poss] but, as can be seen, the engine is quite large and would require a hefty supply of steam and large boiler. Thus, it is only suitable for installing in a very large model.

The small steam engine, whether produced commercially or in the home workshop, has certain features in common. They must all have displacement lubricators to feed oil to the engine to keep the cylinder walls and pistons lubricated. The big end

Fig 11.5 : Vertical fire tube boiler

Fig 11.6 : Typical water tube boiler

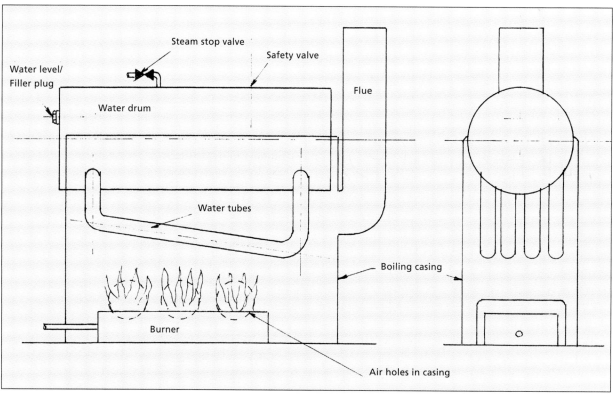

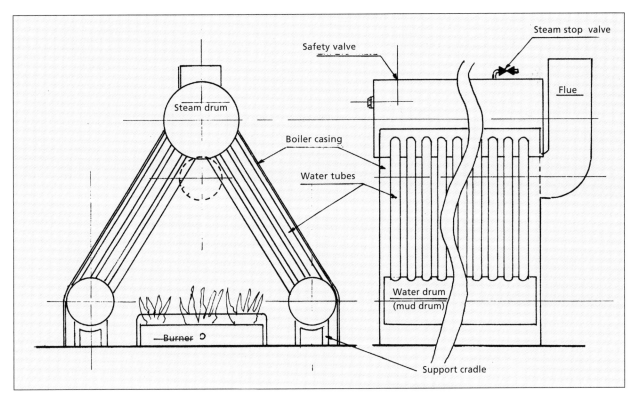

Top Fig 11.7 : Typical three drum watertube boiler

Top Fig 11.8 : Single cylinder oscillating steam engine

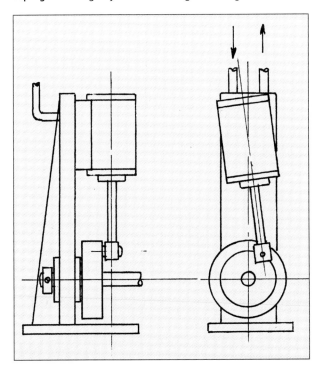

bearings and the main bearings also need to be oiled regularly, as they will not be fed with oil from the displacement lubricator. It is possible to make and fit a small pump to feed oil to the required bearings or to encase the bottom end of the engine in an oil bath but both of these methods seriously increase costs without making a significant improvement over the hand oiling method. The displacement lubricator is shown in Fig. 10/12. Large oscillating engines will generally be fitted with an oil pump, driven off the crankshaft and used to keep the main bearings and big ends oiled.

The slide valve steam engine

The slide valve engine is shown in the sketches and photographs and is the more efficient unit compared to the oscillating engine. In this case, the steam is fed to a steam chest attached to each cylinder, wherein a slide unit driven from an eccentric on the main shaft controls the steam entering and leaving the cylinder. The slide valve is carefully made to allow only the correct amount of steam to enter each cylinder. In turn, this also feeds steam to both ends of the piston so that it is driven in both directions. The slide valve also opens and closes the exhaust port in each steam chest, so that the moving pistons each force the used steam out. These engines need to be carefully timed in a similar manner to timing a car engine. There are a number of ways to reverse a slide valve engine and these are detailed below.

Slide valve engines are made by a number of companies, each of whom have their own selected method of effecting reversing and all can usually be controlled by radio signalled servo units. They usually need two servo units; one to control speed and the second to effect ahead/astern movement. These engines are usually made as in-line units with the cylinders and valve chests all in a single line. It is just about possible to obtain a slide valve engine where the cylinders are set at an angle to each other to form a 'vee', but these are rare. There are also some slide valve engines that have four cylinders and these are generally set in vee formation. The pressure of

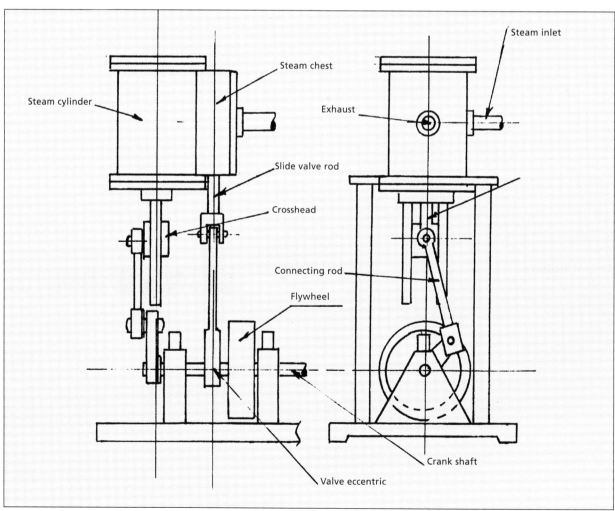

Above: A view of a boiler in the hull of a paddle steamer

Left: Steam boiler with twin gas burners, water gauge, safety valve and pressure gauge with siphon, for supplying steam at up to 70 p.s.ig. to paddle engine.

Fig 11.10 : Simple single cylinder slide valve engine

steam used to drive all these engines will vary from maker to maker. Some, where the engine has fairly big clearances, will run happily with steam at as low as 20 p.s.i.g. (pound-force per square inch gauge), whilst others will need higher pressures up to 70 p.s.i.g. and even higher.

Steam boilers

The model boilers needed for the steam engines described above are comparatively simple but safe units; they certainly bear no resemblance to the boilers in a modern power station or factory plant room which have a comprehensive array of instrumentation and controls to allow serious load fluctuations to be accommodated with minimum delay. They operate at high efficiencies to keep running costs and maintenance costs to a minimum. The boiler for the model tug is neither as efficient nor complex and both firing and running are comparatively simple.

Obviously, all the steam engines described need

suitable boilers to provide steam at the required pressure and so some steam boilers are described here. Basically, there are three types of boiler that can be used in model ships. The first two are both known as shell pattern boilers and comprise vertical and horizontal types. The third pattern is the water tube type and is possibly the most efficient of the three, though very much dependant upon how it is built.

Both vertical and horizontal boilers can be found in a number of configurations and a number are shown in Figs 11/4 to 11/6. On full size steam driven

Deocrated removable paddle box cover on steam driven paddler.

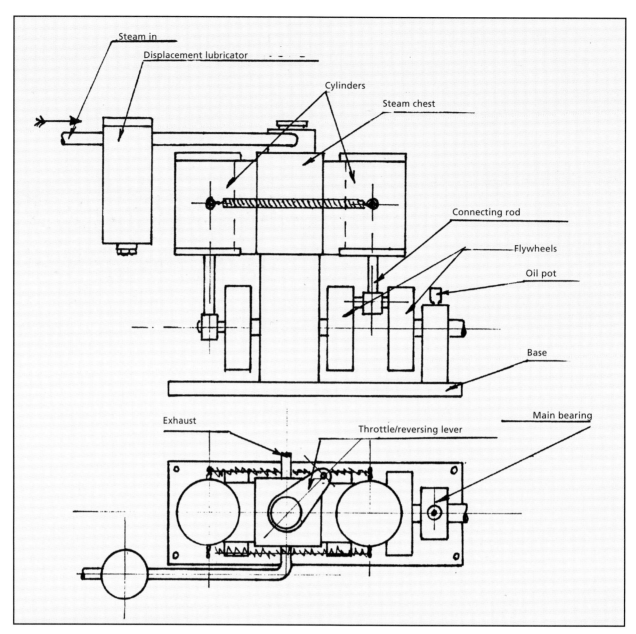

Steam in

Displacement lubricator

Cylinders

Steam chest

Connecting rod

Flywheels

Oil pot

Base

Exhaust

Throttle/reversing lever

Main bearing

Left Fig 11.09 : Typical twin cylinder oscillating steam engine.

Below left: Steam paddle engine installed in model .

Above: Compact arrangement of steam boiler and twin cylinder oscillating engine in a model tug hull engine. *Photo courtesy of Deans Marine*

Below Fig 11.11 : Typical superheater coil for small boiler

Below Fig right 11.12 : Displacement lubricator

tugs horizontal shell boilers, known as 'Scotch boilers', with from one to four cylindrical furnaces according to the size of the boiler were the norm.

By far the simplest boiler for the model tug is made from a single cylinder closed off at each end, set into a basic framework and fired from beneath by a ladder type burner or perhaps, a ceramic radiant panel burner. This boiler being, in essence, a copper tube capped at both ends and fitted with two essentials – a safety valve and a water level plug. Its casing can be of sheet brass or steel – or even tin plate, if adequately insulated – with a means of allowing a burner to be located under the cylinder and an exhaust for the hot gases that can be led into a chimney or funnel. This is

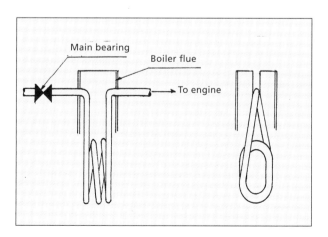

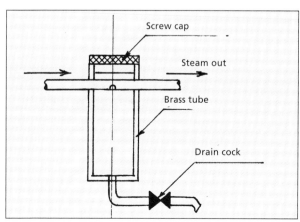

81

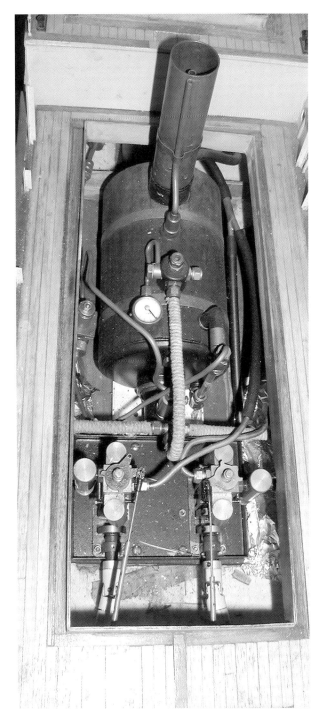

View of twin steam engines in model hull. *Photo courtesy of Deans Marine*

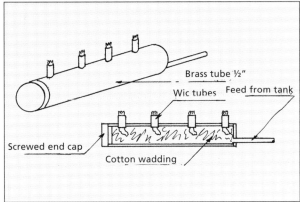

Fig 11.13 : Ladder type spirit burner

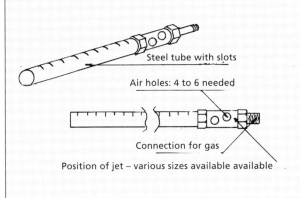

Fig 11.14 : Ladder type gas burner

shown in Fig. 11/8.

Model horizontal boilers usually have only one furnace tube. Sometimes, this passes right through the boiler from front to back but, the more efficient unit has the furnace tube and vertical flue within the boiler shell (Figs 11/2 to 11/4). The vertical boiler has similar variations and the multi-tubular one is usually to be preferred for efficiency.

For rapid steam raising, the water tube pattern boiler is the best, although such a boiler usually requires more space both vertically and in the beam.

As a result, it can be difficult to fit within a given superstructure. Sensibly, a water tube boiler will need to have a pumped water feed system because they have much smaller water spaces than do cylindrical boilers – and so need a constant supply of water to maintain steaming conditions. Water tube boilers of two types are also illustrated. The old working steam tugs almost invariably had Scotch pattern cylindrical boilers and the author has not heard of any British steam tugs that used boilers of the water tube type.

As mentioned briefly before, firing a small steam boiler today is usually done using LPG (liquefied petroleum gas) from small commercially bought cylinders or from purpose made gas tanks filled from commercial cylinders. The best gas is a mix of 30% or 40% propane and 70% or 60% butane. Butane alone tends to cool very rapidly in the tank, when its pressure drops and the burner can fail. So, the mixed gas is preferable and even though it too will cool rapidly, it does produce the hotter flame. In all cases, it is often wise to fit an insulation jacket around the gas tank to prevent it from over-cooling.

It is also possible to fire the small steam boiler quite successfully using methylated spirit and Fig. 11/13 shows how a suitable spirit burner can be made. However, to make such a unit the modeller will need either to be able to work with silver solder for the

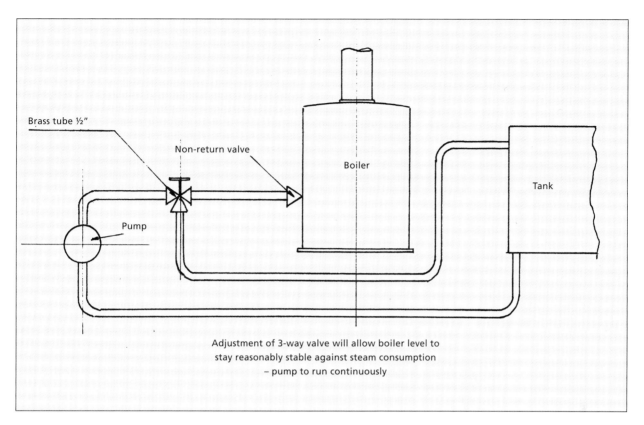

Fig 11.15 : Diagrammatic arrangement of pumped boiler feed system from water tank

Model of compund steam engine under construction to show different cylinder sizes.

various joints in the burner or to enlist the assistance of a suitably skilled friend. At one time, the Japanese maker Seiko marketed a boiler featuring a methylated spirit burner that was quite efficient. Alas, this seems to have disappeared in recent years.

Do please note that steam boilers and gas tanks are pressure vessels which need to be tested and certified if the model is to be run on the public waters of a model boat club. Most local authorities and model clubs require the owners of such pressure vessels to carry insurance against possible damage to third parties and property. When testing fully before it is used, a boiler should be fired up away from anyone and in the open air – never in enclosed premises. The safety aspect of steam boilers and their associated firing equipment cannot be stressed too strongly. Most model ship clubs will have or know of where boiler and gas tank testing can be carried out and certified and such testing must be carried out at intervals of two years. Young children are usually fascinated by any form of moving machinery and enjoy using the 'eyes on the ends of their fingers'. Whilst such youngsters should be kept at a safe distance, this ought not to be to the extent of failing to satisfy their natural curiosity – they are the modellers of tomorrow.

There is something to be said about the romance of steam. The smell of hot oil and burning fuel, to many of us, is as expensive perfume is to the fine lady. It has an ambience that is not found in any other section of model ship building; and once experienced, it is difficult to find in any other place. Like any other aspect of marine modelling, is to be tried when possible and, hopefully, enjoyed.

Chapter 12

Control Equipment

The control equipment top be depends directly and entirely upon what source of power is installed in the tug, i.e. whether an eclectic motor or steam engine.

Electric motors and radio control

If this is the choice, and having decided upon which electric motor(s) to fit and acquired the type of batteries needed to provide the necessary current, the next challenge is to decide how the motor(s) may be controlled from the remote radio system.

Radio control systems currently available to the modeller are described in more detail later in this chapter – but any radio control outfit comprises basically of a transmitter with two or more channels, a receiver, a number of servos and a receiver battery pack with switch harness.

Fig 12.1: Wire wound resistance for speed control

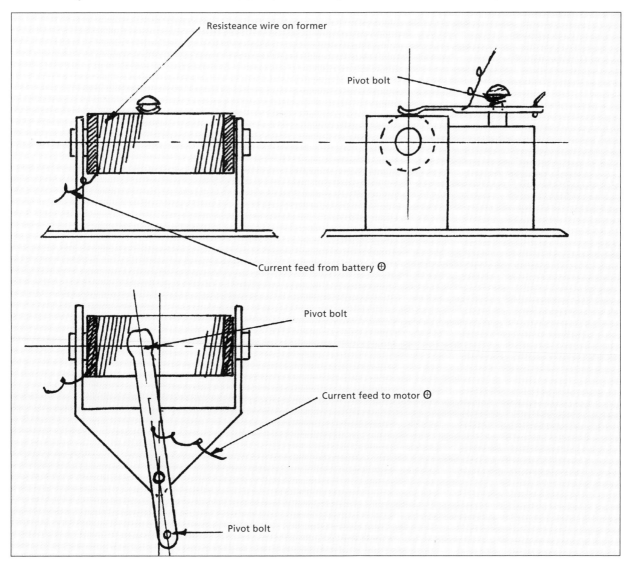

Resisteance wire on former

Pivot bolt

Current feed from battery ⊕

Pivot bolt

Current feed to motor ⊕

Pivot bolt

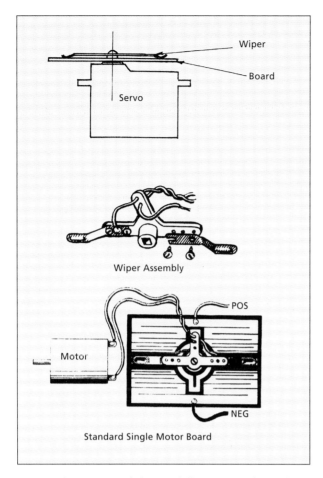

Wiper

Board

Servo

Wiper Assembly

POS

Motor

NEG

Standard Single Motor Board

Left fig 12.2: Typical 'Bobs' board speed control

Right: Control panel for twin screw tug with bow thruster showing electronic speed control units, radio receiver and connections

Below right: Electronic speed controller, radio receiver, battery etc arranged within a single screw tug model.

In order to control the model's motor(s) from the radio equipment, it is essential that the unit installed in the vessel is one that can be operated from a radio signal that fed from the transmitter to the receiver within the model and then be able to use that unit to control the motor(s). This may seem obvious, but it is well worth setting out these basic principles of the operation. Most radio-control outfits have servo units supplied as an inherent part of the unit. These servos, through the signals sent between the transmitter and the receiver, move in a way that mimics the operator's movement of the levers or sticks on the transmitter. Servos can be also be used to operate switches and make limited movements e needed for turning the model's rudder.

Of course, the simplest form of motor control that can be remotely operated is a simple 'on/off 'switch that is linked mechanically to a servo. When the stick on the transmitter is pushed forward, the servo will move as dictated by the receiver and push the switch over to apply power to the motor. Conversely, it will switch off the power when the stick is brought back to its previous 'off' position. However, this is somewhat unsatisfactory and rather rudimentary for use with a scale model, as it simply switches power on or off but provides no way of controlling of speed.

In order to illustrate the workings and use of simple radio control, let us assume that the model is a simple, single-screw tug. One channel of the radio will control the rudder, and thus the direction of the

model, and the other channel will control the speed of the motor via a suitable speed control unit. This is a simple two-channel radio control system in its basic form. The two sticks of the two-channel transmitter provide proportional control through the receiver installed in the model. In turn, this drives servos that operate both the rudder and the equipment that controls the motor direction and speed. Each servo will move only as far as the transmitter stick dictates.

There are a number of very different speed controllers available to the ship modeller, the simplest of which is the resistance type. In this type, a spring-loaded arm is moved by the servo along the surface of a resistor – a coil of resistance wire wound round a rod of insulting (non-conducting) material like hard plastic or similar material. To effect reversal of the motor, the resistance unit general has a central gap and is wired in a manner that will reverse the current direction according to which side of the gap the 'wiper' is moving. This arrangement is shown in the Fig. 12/1.

Only slightly more sophisticated as a control of motor direction and speed is the resistance board, often called Bob's Board. It is readily available from most model shops and by mail order, although becoming less popular as the years pass. It cones in three sizes: up to 2 amps, 2.5-4 amps and 5-7 amps. The board is made from fibreglass, to which continuous strips of resistance material are bonded in a special pattern. The board fits over the servo and twin spring strips are attached to the servo spindle in order that they travel over the resistances as the servo is moved. Connections on the board are wired to the motor and it is controlled both forward and in reverse by the movement of the wipers along the resistor (Fig. 12/2). This pattern of motor controller is possibly the cheapest and simplest on the market and is very reliable, provided it is carefully matched to the current capacity required by the selected motor.

These days, the most popular form of motor control for the marine modeller of is the electronic speed controller (ESC) and manufactured so as to obviate the need for a servo. An ESC will plug directly into the radio receiver in the model and control the speed and direction of the motor in sympathy with the transmitter stick or lever, much in the same manner as the servo moves a wiper over a resistance. The ESC is both much more sophisticated and easier to install in the model, although it can be prone to

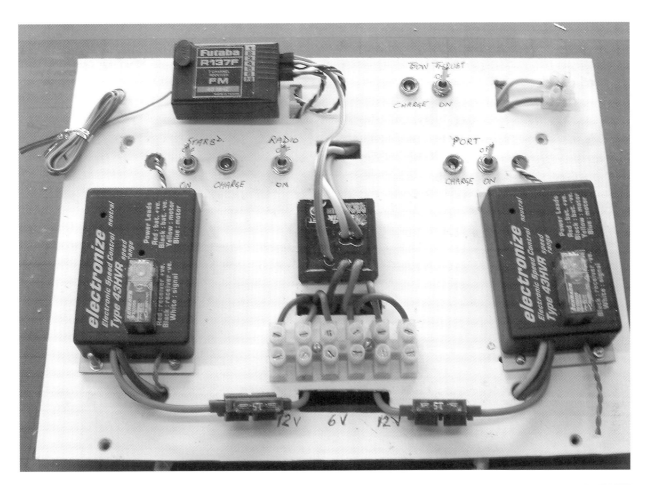

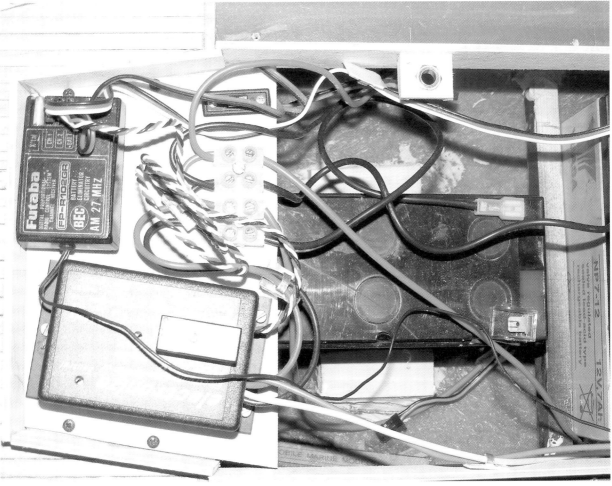

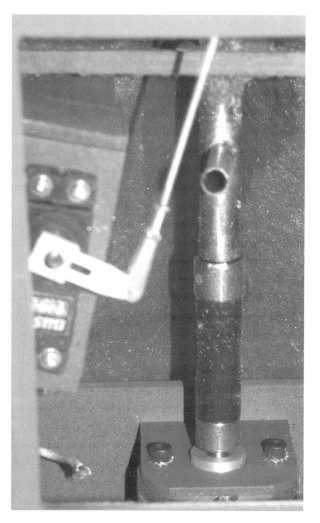

propellers are independently controlled. In this way, the model is more controllable and both turning and running astern are easier to achieve. This type of control usually means that three channels are needed from the radio transmitter; one for the rudder and the other two for control of each motor. Three-channel radio outfits are more readily available today than in the past when two and four channel outfits were the norm. It is possible to purchase an electronic unit that can give a degree of independent control to two motors when using only one channel of the radio. Such a unit will feed two electronic speed controllers from one radio channel with a link to the rudder controller so that when the rudder is turned to the left the left motor will stop and the right screw will speed up to increase the turning moment. Similarly when the rudder turns to the right the left screw will speed up and the right motor will stop to increase the turn. A two-channel radio will thus control the twin-screw vessel saving the difference in cost between the three or four channel radio and the two-channel unit except for the cost of the splitter unit. While the above method can show a saving over the multi-channel radio system one should remember that the multi channel system does offer the means to remotely

Detail of propeller shaft with oiler tube and coupling together with offset servo for rudder control.

Twin servo units for controlling model steam plant.

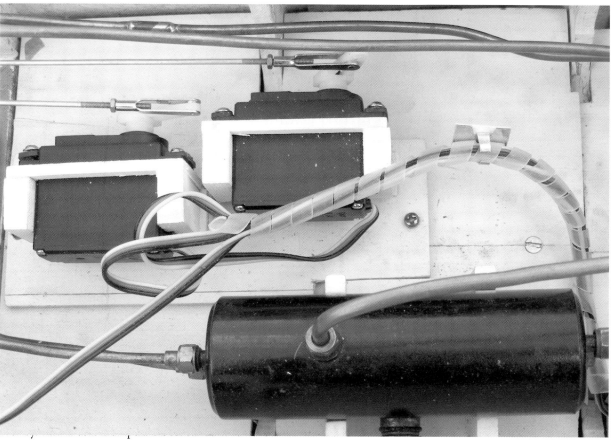

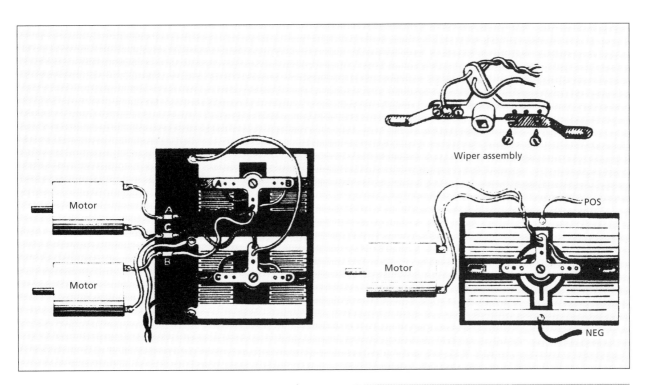

Fig 12.3: Arrangement of 'Bobs' board for twin motor control.

Right: Digital test meter very useful for testing and checking installation of electrical and electronic equipment.

Below: Analogue test meter. Both meters illustrated are inexpensive and a valuable addition to the model tug builders tool kit.

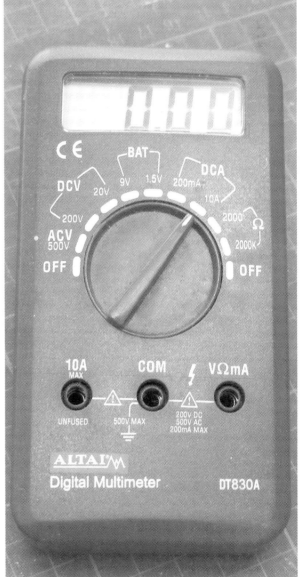

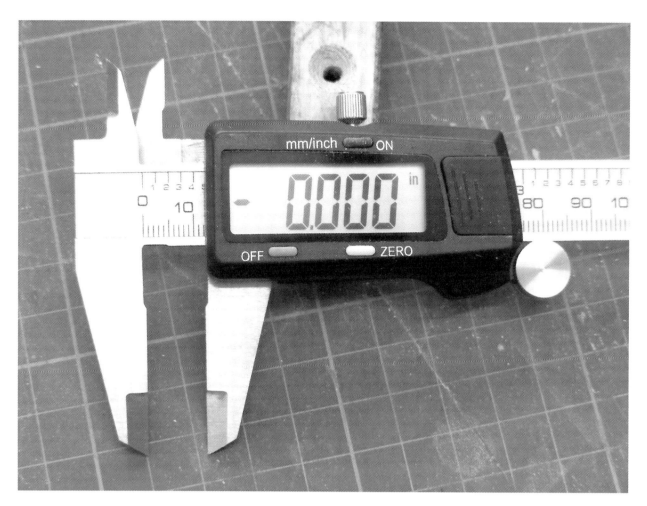

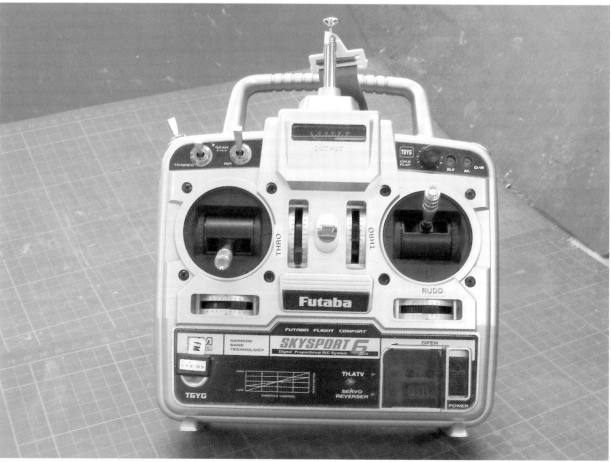

Left: Digital callipers with electronic readout. Useful for accurately measuring.

Left below: Futaba Skysport 6 six-channel radio transmitter for use on 40 Mhz range and ideal for radio control of multi screw model tugs.

Above: Hi-tec Zebra two-channel radio transmitter unit, possibly one of the cheapest units available but very suitable for controlling the single screw model.

operate auxiliary functions such a smoke, sound, lights, etc.

The modeller should be aware that the location of electronic control units within the hull must be carefully considered. The resistance controller can become quite hot when in use and thus needs to be positioned where cooling air can flow over. Also, whilst many ESCs have built-in heat sinks, some degree of airflow is still desirable. Even more sophisticated are the ESCs with controller casings designed to permit them to be water cooled. Units like these need to be installed with associated pipework and water scoops beneath the hull, the scoops being arranged to direct the cooling water correctly.

In all cases, speed controllers need to be installed where they can easily be removed for attention, in an area that has a free airflow and where there is little chance of water splashing over them. As with all electrical and electronic equipment, water does them no good at all!

Remember too that all controllers and servos draw current from the receiver battery pack – so that when the battery runs low control of the model can be lost. For lengthy running sessions, it is wise to fit a receiver battery pack of a higher rating than that usually supplied with the radio outfit. The standard radio battery pack is usually rated at 500 milli-amp hours, but packs rated at up to 2000 milli-amp hours or more can be found and they will increase the running time available appreciably.

Some ESCs have a feature known as a BEC (battery eliminator circuit) that allows power for the radio and its attachments to be taken from the main drive battery, thereby allowing the receiver battery pack to be omitted. Whether this is an advantage or not is a matter of personal opinion. In a model having a limited amount of internal space, the elimination of the radio battery pack may be a serious advantage, as it will when the model is needed to run in trials of some duration and where could be a significant saving.

On the other hand, the radio signal will be lost if the battery were to run low, will receiver battery pack in the same circumstances; and, of course, a low main battery means that the model will fail in the middle of the lake, with all the attendant recovery problems.

Radio receiver and electronic speed controller within the hull of a single screw tug.

The author has built a number of models where the radio system has incorporated the BEC system of the controllers and they have proved to be very reliable and satisfactory. As is to be found with all radio equipment, advances in electronics today means that items bought today may well be out of date tomorrow.

The four-channel radio outfit is possibly the most commonly used system today. It offers not only control of rudder and two motors, but also has the advantage of a fourth channel that can be used to operate a number of auxiliary features. This fourth channel, controlled from one of the sticks on the transmitter, can be adapted by the use of switching units, to switch lights on and off, to operate smoke generators and to operate other units that can be simply switched. The fourth channel can also be used to operate a bow thruster unit that will aid the turning of the model in tight situations. All of these features enhance substantially the use and enjoyment of the model tug.

There are also transmitter units that have five and even six channels; and others that can accept electronic switch panels. These panels have a great many on/off functions, all of which can, when necessary, provide additional switching facilities.

Remote control of model ships has been commonplace for many years and has become ever more sophisticated – and, thankfully, more reliable. Just as the personal and home computer

has improved, so has the radio control system. So, in many ways it has become easier to operate, even though, to many of us, seeming ever more complex internally. The author admits cheerfully to being one of those marine modellers who does not understand the insides of his radios, but who is happy to have the expert provide help and instruction. As a result these notes are the combined work of lots of welcome advice from far too many to be named, but whose efforts have been translated with gratitude to the simplistic work here.

The most common radio controls for model tugs in the UK are set to operate within the two frequency bands of 27 and 40 megahertz (written as 27 MHz and 40 MHz) but often spoken as '27 meg', '40 meg', etc.) and the number of individual frequency channels within these bands is detailed in Appendix 3.

In the U.K., the use of other frequencies, such as 35 MHz as used by model aircraft, is illegal. In other parts of the world, different frequencies apply and the operator in each country must adhere to the allocated frequency bands, within each of which there are a number of channels. In the 27-MHz band, the channels are delineated by colour, whereas in the 40-MHz band, they are given a three figure number

Further view of above tug interior.

coding (see Appendix 3).

The control crystals in both transmitter and receiver are pre-set to one of these band channels, so that more than one model can be sailed at a time, that is as long as each model uses a different channel. Because of this, it is important when visiting the sailing pond or lake to ensure that the crystal in use does not conflict with that of any other user. If it does, then the crystals must be changed or the modeller must wait until the channel becomes free before sailing the model. Most model boat clubs have a frequency board displayed at the water side with the number of channels in each band being indicated by means of coloured and numbered spring clothes pegs. Each individual user obtains the peg applicable to his/her frequency and clips this to the transmitter aerial. The fact that the peg is missing from the frequency board indicates that the particular channel is in use and may not be used by anyone until the peg is returned. This is the accepted and universally used system among model boat clubs in the U.K, and similar systems are in use in other countries.

The simplest control outfit is the two-channel radio system. Usually, it comprises a transmitter (usually referred to as a Tx), a receiver (the Rx), two servo units, a receiver battery holder and a switch harness.

In addition, there are usually a number of different horns and discs that can be fitted to the servo drive shafts. The types of horns and discs illustrated are used to connect the servo to the part of the model that is to be controlled.

The Tx requires batteries to be slotted into the casing. Generally, eight AA size batteries are needed – although some transmitters are supplied with rechargeable battery units already installed. On the front of the Tx are two control sticks or levers. The one to the left usually moves up and down and the one on the right moves left to right. Both sticks are self-centring, but can generally be fitted with ratchets to allow them to stay in a set place when required. As designed, the left stick is used for speed and direction of the drive motor or engine, and the right stick is designed to control the rudder for steering.

Also positioned on the front of the transmitter is an on/off switch and a meter or coloured light system to indicate the charge state of the battery pack. The Tx crystal itself s generally located in an easily accessible place, as is the charging socket for the batteries. Note that the crystal for the Tx is usually slightly different from that of the Rx in order to ensure that they are fitted to the correct unit; and both will carry labels indicating the frequency for which they are designed.

The receiver supplied with the two-channel outfit will have three sockets at one end; one accepts the

Left: Low speed, high torque 12v. motor.

Below: 4-Channel 40 megH radio receiver by Futaba.

the aerial always remains as supplied. As it is often difficult to find a suitable location for a long aerial lead on the model, it is quite sensible to run the wire around the top of the inside of the main deck. There it will remain effective over reasonable distances – although it is always wise to check the effectiveness of the radio installation before taking a model to the water for the first time.

The Rx needs to be protected from water and, particularly in the case of a steam driven model from

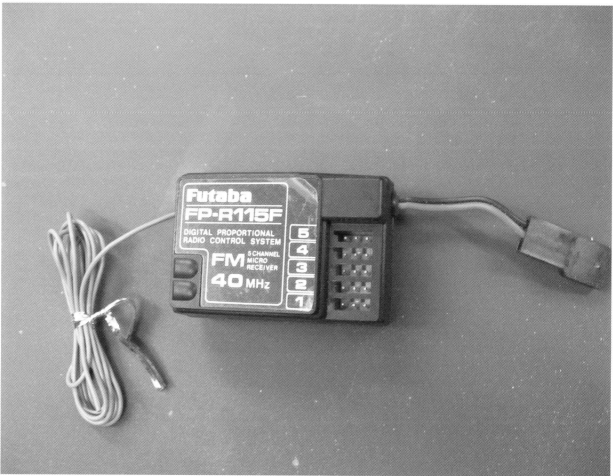

battery connection and the others to accept the connections from the servos, or a servo, and an ESC. A long, single aerial cable will usually exit from the opposite end to the sockets. Some receivers have aerial leads that measure as much as a meter in length (over three feet), whilst others have aerial leads of only 50 cm (about 18 inches). Overall, under no circumstances should the length of the receiver aerial be shortened or lengthened as they are carefully matched to suit the signals of the Tx. Any alteration to the length will affect the operation of the system. It is possible to use a section of the rigging of a model as an aerial, provided that the rigging is made from the right type of wire and that the total length of

the steam. Placing the Rx in a small plastic box or similar damp-proof container, with the aerial and other leads running out through protective sleeves, is a simple solution. The battery pack associated with the Rx is usually designed to accept 4 x AA size cells. Alternatively, it may be a rechargeable pack. Whichever, the battery pack is connected to the Rx by a small wiring harness incorporating a small switch and, in the case of a rechargeable pack, with a charging connection. The battery pack can be fitted into the same box as the receiver, with the switch fitted through the lid - and many modellers have used some rather clever means of disguising the switch when fitted through the deck of a model.

The four-channel and multi-channel radio outfits are similar to the two-channel unit described above, and follow similar rules. They are supplied with varying numbers of servo units and will thus have differing costs. Almost all will have two sticks on the front of the transmitter, where each stick will control two functions instead of only one. Each stick can move up or down, and left or right, so that they can operate two servos or other units each. Rx will have more sockets to accept more servos or ESCs, but will have a similar aerial lead to that of the two-channel unit, The battery pack and switch harness but there will usually be a similar to those already described.

Many of these multi-channel outfits can be adapted to accept switching units in order to give a great many more remote operations remotely. The modeller wishing to go down this road will need to seek advice from the supplier/model shop or from an experienced modeller at the local model boat club. Limitations of space here prevent the author for doing more than point the way.

The three-channel outfit will happily cope with two motor controls and a rudder, giving the tug builder the facility of having independent twin-screw control. The four-channel outfit will add the extra channel which allows the builder to add an additional remotely operation function – such as lights or creating smoke. The multi-channel outfit extends the facilities even further to other remotely controlled functions. However, each additional function will, obviously, increase cost – and can increase the possibility of extra problems arising. So, the prospective tug modeller needs to look at both aspects and balance cost against complexities.

In recent years, the very latest radio control systems to appear featuring mainly systems that do not have crystals and can be programmed to suit a number of models from the Tx, with each model being suitably coded. These outfits operate on the higher frequency of 2.4 GHz (2.4 Gigahertz) and have been the subject of some controversy. The most obvious aspect of these units is the fact that their aerials, both for the Tx and for the Rx, are very short – about 3-4 inches long (80-100 mm). This is a consequence of the fact that their high frequency is located within the microwave band. Actually, the receiver (Rx) has two aerials, one horizontal and one vertical, that also need to be in those same configurations on the model itself.

With these outfits, each maker's system generally operates over 80 frequencies and the Tx randomly selects two clear channels and locks on to them. There are apparent differences between the systems used by the makers – Futaba, Spektrum and J.R. – and there are other outfits still under development. Like most newly developed systems, there are advantages and disadvantages; so the modeller needs to seek advice from the vendors and select the system that best suits his/her needs.

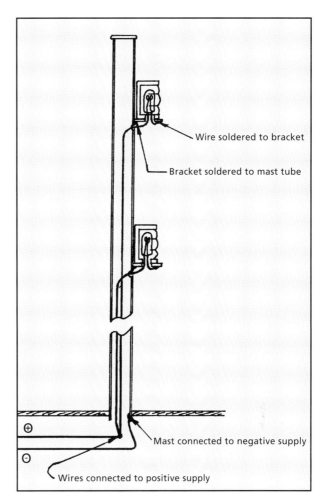

Fig 12.4: Wiring for twin lights on single tubular mast.

However, the biggest advantage that comes immediately to mind for these new systems is that there is no need to select a channel peg from the board at the water side, or to search for that elusive crystal not already in use, before one can sail the latest model tug. As explained earlier, the author is no expert in electronics and depends upon the information fed to readers in the model boat magazines each month. Nevertheless, the 2.4 GHz outfits do seem to be comparatively easy to set up and their accompanying instruction books provide reasonably clear instructions regarding the setting-up operation.

As with all radio systems, the Tx aerial length is critical and alterations to such lengths can seriously affect the operation of the system. This seems to be even more important with the 2.4 GHz systems and so range tests need to be carried out. Any modeller proposing to use this equipment would be well advised to read up on this material beforehand. Some excellent and informative articles appeared in 2008 in both Model Boats and Marine Modelling International magazines and back issues can be obtained if details of the appropriate magazines are specified (the Model Boats notes can be found in the May, October and November 2008 issues and in the September and October 2008 issues of Marine Modelling). Obviously, the makers of such radio equipment have brochures and leaflets that will also assist the modeller and these will be found at the outlets marketing the radio systems. As a start, any good ship model shop will, almost certainly, carry brochures and information on these new 2.4 GHz outfits and the prospective user should research all available advice and information very seriously before committing his/her hard earned cash.

Steam outfits

Quite simply, the control of the model steam engine and boiler is down to servo motor drives. Some steam outfits combine speed and direction in one lever, so that speed and direction need only one servo and a simple two-channel radio control outfit will suffice. Some need one servo driving the valve controlling the steam to the engine (speed) and another servo driving the lever that controls the ahead/astern movement. As a result, a three-channel outfit is needed here and twin-screw outfits with twin engines will obviously, need even more channels.

Cheddar Models – who are sadly no longer in business – produced a system of controlling electronically both the boiler feed water supply and the boiler pressure automatically; and the author successfully applied this system to two models. At the time of writing, Cheddar Models steam outfits are now being supplied by Stuart Models (see Appendix 2), but they do not expect to offer their version of the automatic boiler control system until some time in the future. However, they do produce a simple, automatic burner control linking boiler pressure to burner in order to modulate the gas flow in sympathy with the boiler pressure.

The tug modeller using steam propulsion would be well advised to take the time needed to become proficient in the handling of his/her tug. Steam drives can be very powerful when correctly installed and fitted, but the modeller needs to have practice before running such a tug in competition. When the tug is required to tow heavy un-powered models, then the slide-valve operated, twin-cylinder engine is the best unit to install. The author's experiences with small oscillating steam engines is that they perform well, but have less power available than does a slide-valve engine of the same cylinder size.

Chapter 13

Deck Details and Machinery

The decks of most tugs, ancient or modern, carry a plethora of fittings and machinery and the location detail of such machinery is relative to its duties. In the early tugs, the most important item was probably the tow hook(s). After all, these early vessels were little more than a fairly small hull, with basic superstructure and a powerful engine – usually the largest engine and boiler plant that could be accommodated. So, the tow hook is perhaps the best place at which to start looking at deck fittings.

Over time, the design of tow hooks developed only slowly – so that even today, those installed on a modern tug are very little different to those of years ago. Three patterns of tow hooks are illustrated here, with the Liverpool pattern possibly being the most common. They were invariably fitted upon a substantial structure aft of the main superstructure and, in virtually all cases, each hook incorporated a heavy spring tat acted as a shock absorber. In addition, almost all tow hooks were also fitted with a latch that could be set to prevent the tow rope from being slipped accidentally. When the latch was manually lifted, the hook could drop and the rope would be released.

Tow hook and detail on model tug. *Photo courtesy of Model Slipway.*

Larger tugs generally carried two tow hooks that were supported on a semicircular frame as can be seen here in the accompanying photographs. These hooks had to be very carefully made. Initially, they were made of cast iron, but later vessels had hooks cast in steel. Both types were mounted on very heavy plating and the location for the hook would be generally strengthened and arranged, so that the strain of the tow was taken by the structure of the ship.

Model tow hooks can be found within the manufacturer's catalogues. Many are cast in white metal and others in hard plastic – so the modeller can generally find a suitable tow hook in the scale being used. For the model tug to be used in towing competitions then the hook cast in white metal or hard plastic is unsuitable and the modeller will have to find an alternative or make one specifically. Mobile Marine Models (see Appendix 2) make a working tow hook that needs to be mounted on to a strengthened deck, where the weight of the tow will be spread over a wide area of the hull and deck. The keen modeller can, of course, make a suitable hook using brass rod. It will have to be shaped after it has been annealed and its installation should suit the model appropriately.

Winches

The modern tug, although almost always having a tow hook, will rely mainly upon a large towing winch. Using a winch, the tow can be drawn close to the tug or let out, so that the tow is a long way from the tug and with the winch being operated remotely from the wheelhouse.

The majority of winches designed for towing are hydraulically operated. Where there is only one winch, it is generally mounted aft of the tug's

Compact hydraulic winch by Mobile Marine Models..

Twin combined winch/windlasses on Ayton Cross courtesy Mobile marine Mode

superstructure with a section of the upper deck forming a shelter over the winch. There are a number of tugs where there is not only a winch aft of the structure, but also one or two, possibly slightly smaller, towing winches on the fore deck to

Fig 13.1: Typical hydraulic towing winch.

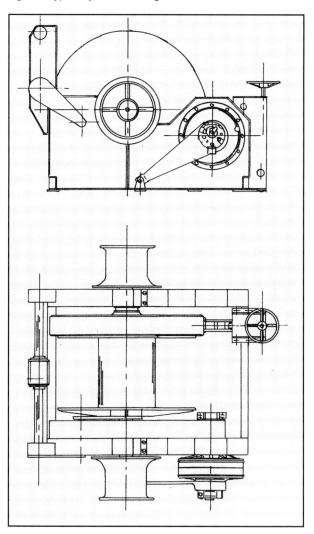

Twin winches by Mobile Marine Models.

allow the tug to tow backwards as well as forwards. This arrangement is well illustrated here in the photographs of the model tug Ayton Cross.

Powered winches for rope handling and working with derricks and with mooring ropes can, of course, be powered by steam, electrically or hydraulically. Steam was once the source of power on all steam-driven tugs almost without exception, although electric drive was sometimes used where the generation capacity was adequate. Electric drive became increasingly popular with the advent of the diesel-driven tug – though, these days, the use of hydraulic power seems to run parallel with that of electricity.

The size and complexity of the towing winch is directly proportional to the tug's duty and although the winch for towing is now common practice, the

Fig 13.2: Standard capstan with cable gypsy.

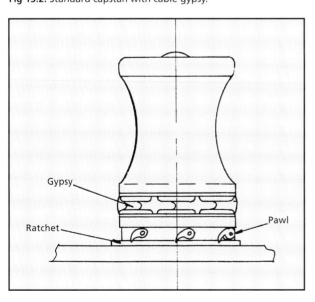

Combined winch and windlass by Mobile Marine Models.

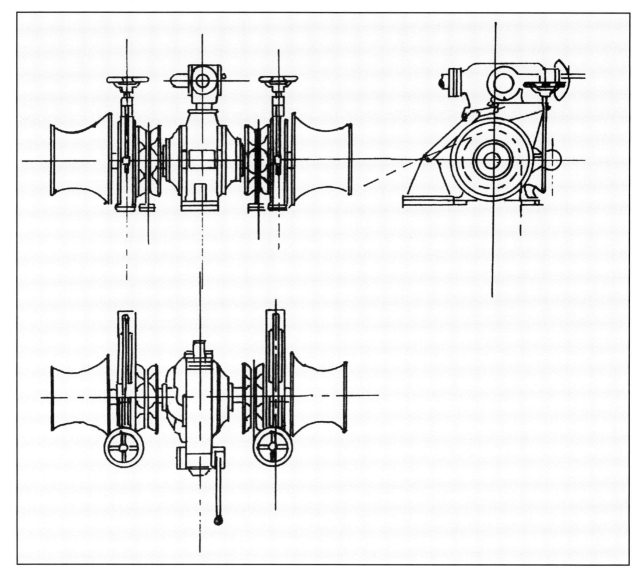

Fig 13.3: Hydraulic windlass with two gypsies.

Detail of double drum towing winch for model tug. Photo courtesy of Model Slipway.

tow hook remains an active feature of all tugs. Some towing winches are illustrated. Towing winches have the large diameter drums that are needed to carry the long lengths of specially produced steel wire cable. One of the photographs here shows a tug loading a new tow cable from a quayside drum immediately astern.

When towing for long distances tugs generally have the tow as far astern as is feasible – maybe half-a-mile (around 1 km) or more, with the towing cable often sinking under the surface. Although steel cable is used, there will generally be a length of sisal or nylon rope between the wire and the towed vessel. This acts as a shock absorber, steel wire rope having much less intrinsic elasticity than sisal or nylon. In addition, a modern towing winch has an inbuilt degree of shock absorbency and its main advantage is that the tow cable can be drawn in or let out to suit the towing conditions.

It is possible for the tug modeller to purchase small winch kits and some manufacturers carry a range of such kits that may be assembled into very accurate replicas of the real unit. The discerning modeller will select carefully from such offerings in order to ensure that the finished model winch is accurate in scale. Some more enterprising tug model builders have fitted working towing winches to their vessels and use these with success when competing in competitions.

Two other items of machinery – as distinct from fittings – are to be found on tugs: the capstan and the windlass. The former is used generally for rope haulage and the latter for handling the anchors.

Capstans

Stern deck detail on tug showing hatch, vent and capstan etc. Photo courtesy of Mobile Marine Models.

Almost all tugs will have a capstan of some sort for handling ropes when the tug is berthing, or for handling rope between the vessel being towed and the tug. In effect, the capstan is a vertical warping drum, usually driven from beneath by a constant speed motor. The operator winds a turn or two of rope round the drum and by pulling on it manually uses the power of the drum to pull the rope while he guides it. Capstans can be driven by steam or electricity, or sometimes driven hydraulically. Diagrams (Fig. 13/1) include details to assist the model builder and capstans can also be seen in the photographs.

Windlasses

The windlass should not be confused with the winch; many modellers call the anchor windlass a winch incorrectly. The windlass does not have a rope drum, but instead has a so-termed 'gypsy', or two, that are designed to hold the links of the anchor cable (chain) and used to raise or lower the anchors when necessary. Both windlasses and winches may have warping drums for rope haulage; but the windlass is

Manually operated windlass for small tug model. Photo by Mobile Marine Models.

Hydraulic windlass for model tug by Mobile Marine Models.

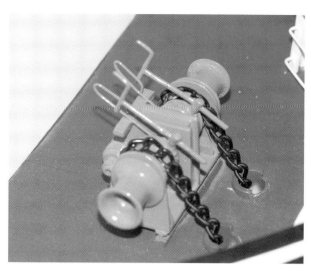

Model windlass as fitted to tug 'AFON ALAW'.

not designed to wind and store rope on a drum.

As with winches, windlasses on steam ships were steam operated, but could also be electrically or hydraulically driven. Examples of windlasses are shown here both photographically and in the diagrams (Figs 13/2 and 13/3). In the same way that winches are to be found in the ranges of fittings from most kit makers, windlasses are also available. They greatly enhance a kit and, with care, some can be motorised and arranged to raise or lower the model anchor – that is, provided the selected anchor is

reasonably weighty. Windlasses are usually found only on the fore deck of the tug, where they are instantly visible. As a result, and in order to avoid glaring inaccuracies, they need to be modelled with care. A badly made model windlass is identified much more quickly than is a winch, the latter often being partly hidden by rigging and other deck fittings.

Foredeck detail of model tug 'MOORCOCK' showing electric windlass etc. Photo by Ray Brigden.

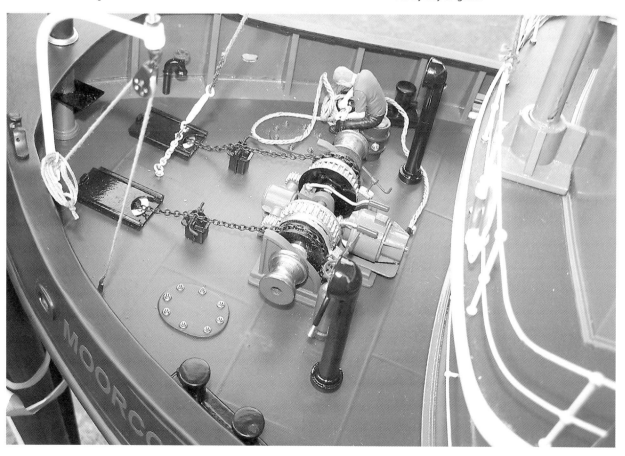

Cranes

Many tugs today, even relatively small ones have hydraulic cranes on their stern deck, usually located close to the main deck housing. They can vary in size, both with the tug and with the duty for the work they do, and are used for anchor handling, rope handling and similar duties. Depending upon the pattern of crane fitted, modellers can build their own, or can choose to purchase a suitable model from the ranges produced by the model manufacturers. It may be possible to find a suitable model crane (or a kit from which to build one) from the ranges made for model railway enthusiasts – and so the discerning modeller will research all sources diligently. Photographs of two kinds of hydraulic cranes are included here.

Fig 13.4 Samson post pattern crane with derrick.

Ventilators

Virtually all tugs have some form of ventilation in order to allow stale air to be evacuated or to let clean air enter spaces below deck. On the earliest tugs, the ventilation was generally primitive and little more than requiring that engine room skylights were fixed in the open position, with some hatches also fixed open – even in poor weather. The cowl ventilator, illustrated here, was designed specifically to aid ventilation of below deck spaces. When faced into the wind, it could be used to feed in fresh air; faced away from the wind, it drew out stale air. In its way, for its time, it was fairly efficient and is to be found in very nearly all kinds of ships, including tugs, up to the present day. Some cowl vents have been fitted with electrically driven fans to increase their efficiency.

Cowl vents were, and still are, made to comply with ship Classification Society requirements, with their

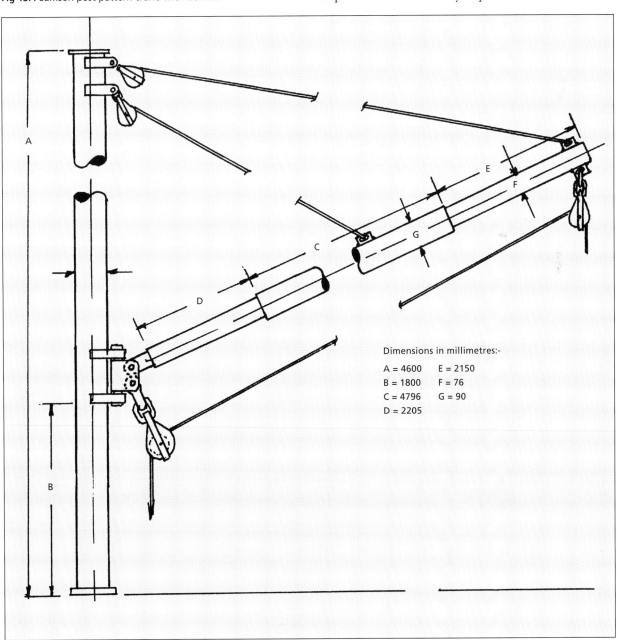

Dimensions in millimetres:-

A = 4600   E = 2150
B = 1800   F = 76
C = 4796   G = 90
D = 2205

Left: Work in progress on tug 'AFON BRAINT' illustrating crane, towing winch etc.

Below left: Model of Hydraulic crane for tug 'AFON ALAW'.

Detail of after deck crane etc on a model tug. Photo courtesy of Model Slipway.

Right Fig 13.5: Cowl pattern ventilator.

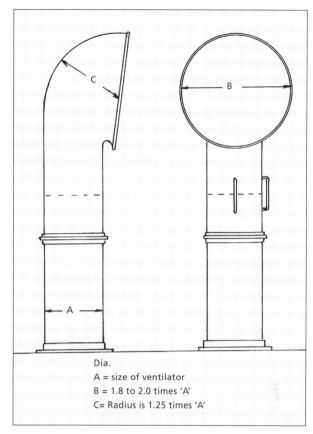

Dia.
A = size of ventilator
B = 1.8 to 2.0 times 'A'
C = Radius is 1.25 times 'A'

cowl and trunk size all calculated to give maximum effect. On steam-driven tugs, especially, one or more of the cowl vents usually had a hoist built inside in order to allow ash from the boilers to be lifted to deck level and thrown overboard – a small hatch in the trunk of the ventilator above deck being installed for this purpose. The next development, following the cowl vent, was the mushroom ventilator, shaped as its names implies, like mushroom. The majority were static units, the curved top cover serving to keep out waves or rainwater or waves, although later units incorporated fans to increase their efficiency.

They are easy to model from short pieces of pipe used in two sizes and with a disc of flat material for a top. The development of ventilation systems ashore

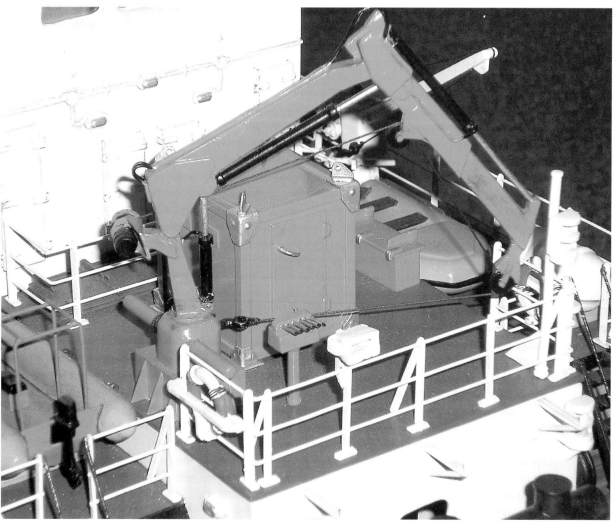

led to the revision of onboard ventilation and the use of fans – forced ventilation systems -– to force air into the spaces between decks and into cabin spaces became more common. Virtually all ships had generators of one kind or other and so the power available allowed electric fans to supersede the steam driven fans of earlier days.

The first attempts at feeding air into accommodation using ducts with outlets and incorporating dampers were attributed to the Thermotank Company. Their system involved installing a fan room at high level on the ship. The fans both feed in fresh air and also extract foul air. They can also incorporate a heating element (radiator) within the input ducting to providing the accommodation with central heating. To this day, a fan room like this is referred to commonly as 'the Thermotank room'. Naturally, the same system has been developed to provide a ship with complete air conditioning.

Beneath decks, and within the double bottom of the tug, lie the tanks that are needed to carry water, fuel oil and waste. All need to be ventilated and to have air enter in order to replace liquids when drawn away, or to have air displaced when they are filled with liquid. As a result, vents of differing patterns are usually sited around the perimeter of the deck and within the protection of the bulwarks and bulwark rails. The simplest type of vent is of the goose neck pattern and which is simply a piece of pipe curved at the top to point down to the deck where air can enter

Above: Guard rails also illustrating gooseneck vent.

Right: Close up of rail with gooseneck vent.

Below: Alternate arrangement of rails with vent in place

or leave, but where it will be difficult for water to enter. Others have patented tops for the same purpose and others incorporate the means of accepting a dip rod to verify the depth of the tank contents. The most sophisticated of all allow for the movement of air and incorporate a remote sensing system to indicate the quantity of liquid in the tank. Most types are illustrated here.

Bollards, fairleads, etc.

All tugs have bollards for tying off ropes. In the main, these are mooring ropes, but the bollards are also used for securing other ropes when necessary. They are of single, double or treble post pattern and are made to sizes and under the rules of the Classification Societies and a table is given in Fig.13.8 covering one type of double post bollard – and they are also illustrated in the deck detail photographs. All types and sizes of bollards will be found in the catalogues of the model ship kit manufacturers, and there is a huge selection covering almost all accepted scales.

It is possible, of course, for the modeller to make

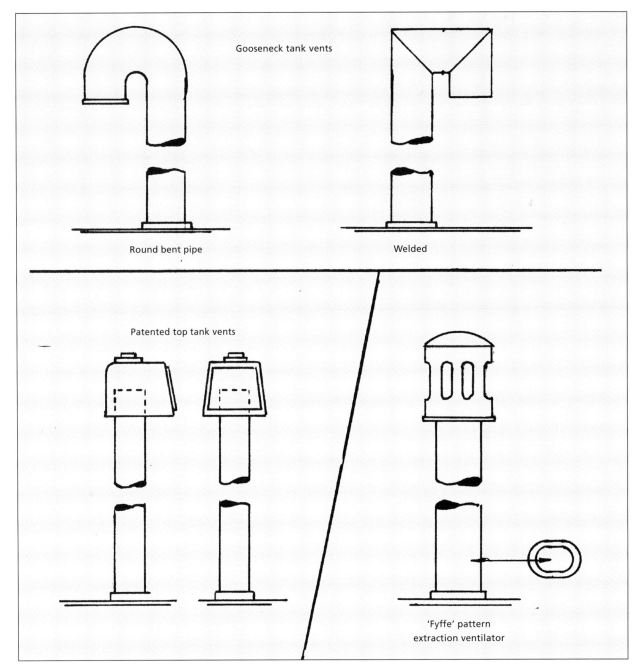

Gooseneck tank vents

Round bent pipe

Welded

Patented top tank vents

'Fyffe' pattern
extraction ventilator

Fig 13.6: Standard tank vents

them within the workshop. The easiest made by the author uses plastic knitting needles for the columns and pieces of styrene sheet from which to cut the necessary bases. Knitting needles are sold in metric sizes and are precisely the diameter indicated on the packaging. They are easily cut to the required lengths and using a letter punch or similar instrument, small bollard tops can be made from discs of styrene cut from thin sheet. Fitted together with thin 'Superglue' and painted upon completion, they are very inexpensive to make, given the quantity that a can be made from a single pair of knitting needles.

It should be noted that the plate bulwarks of a real tug will often be cut away where bollards are sited in order to permit easy passage for the ropes. A fair number of tugs also have bollards specially made to suit a particular location and some are illustrated here. In such instances, the tug modeller should research the actual vessel that

the model is to depict; and a selection of photographs of the real tug will always help with this task.

Fairleads are designed to guide ropes and hawsers from one position to another as well as to reduce the possible frictional wear on the rope. They come in many forms; some are simply cast units carefully ground smooth for the passage of the rope, while others incorporate small pulleys that revolve with the rope and ease its route. As with all deck fittings, fairleads are covered by the rules of the appropriate Classification Society. Many model kit makers carry fairleads of differing types and sizes in their ranges of fittings; or, if necessary, the tug modeller can make them from scrap material in the workshop. A number are illustrated here (Figs. 13/9 and 13/10).

Bow deck details of model tug 'AYTON CROSS'

One unit which can be classed as a fairlead is known as a Panama port. This is a unit generally made of cast metal and welded into a hole that has been cut in the bulwark plating of the tug. It provides a smooth surface over which the rope can run and so helps to reduce wear. A typical Panama port is shown in Fig. 13/9 . As for other fittings, some kit makers include Panama port fittings within their lists and the modeller can select those needed by reference to scale and appearance. They can, like most fittings, be made in model form, but need some care in shaping using small files and fine sand paper.

Chains

Chains do need to be considered carefully when part of a model. The chains that are used to raise and lower a tug's anchors are called cables. They are chains with links that are barred to give greater strength. Barred cable is clearly shown in some of the photographs of real tugs. Modelling chain like this has not been available commercially until comparatively recently but can now be found in a few sizes within the lists of some suppliers. So, up until this time, most tug modellers wishing to show a correctly barred chain cable were required to make it themselves. It was an onerous job, requiring each link to be formed and joined to its neighbour very carefully. Many modellers who continue to make their own will often use plain link chain for anchor cable, However, it can be seen readily that this is be incorrect as it is a highly visible item on the tug's foredeck and where it is running over the gypsies of windlass.

Plain link chain is, however, used in many places on the model tug. Where very fine chain is needed, a costume jewellery shop will probably have a suitable supply. (This is by far the best source of supply. It is definitely not a good idea to raid the jewellery boxes of the spouse or lady of the house for such chain; such action could be misinterpreted with dire results!)

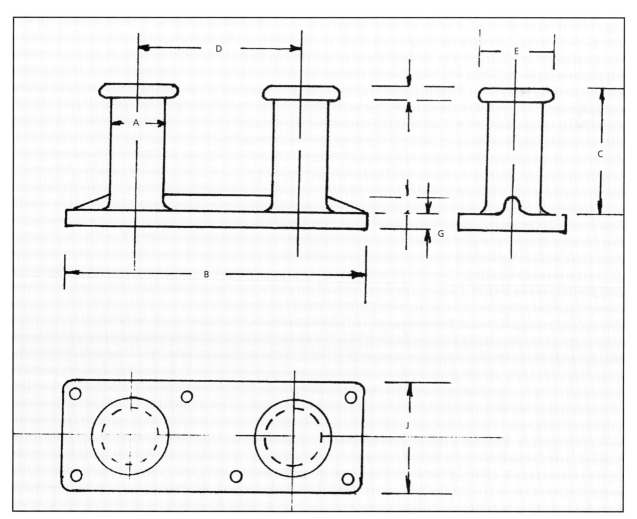

Size	A	B	C	D	E	F	G	J
1	114	600	200	350	145	10	100	210
2	168	800	275	500	205	10	100	260
3	219	950	350	600	255	10	100	330
4	273	1150	400	750	320	10	110	370
5	324	1350	475	900	370	12	110	420
6	356	1500	535	1000	405	12	110	470
7	406	1650	600	1100	450	14	125	540

All dimensions in millimetres

Fig 13.08: Size table for double bollards.

General deck fittings

If one examines the general arrangement drawings and photographs of a full size tug, one will find a wealth of fittings and structures that have not yet been mentioned. For example, hatches abound on most tugs; they give access to the interior of sections of the tug that are not large enough to have companionways and full size doors. They are usually quite simply a square or rectangular coaming with a lid and located over an entrance to an under-deck compartment. Such hatches give access to chain lockers, engine rooms and storage spaces. They are easily make for any model – from scraps of plywood, styrene or even

from small blocks of wood – and can be suitably detailed with hinges, handle or a hand wheel. Some can be seen in the deck detail photograph.

As the name suggests, skylights are shaped units that allow light into spaces beneath the deck; and

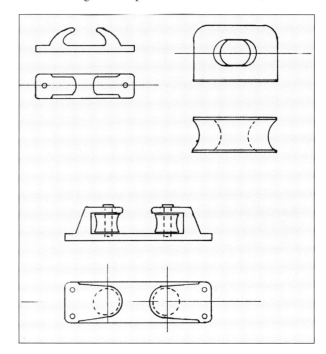

Fig 13.10: A range of typical fairleads.

Fig 13.9: Oval mooring pipe or fairlead.

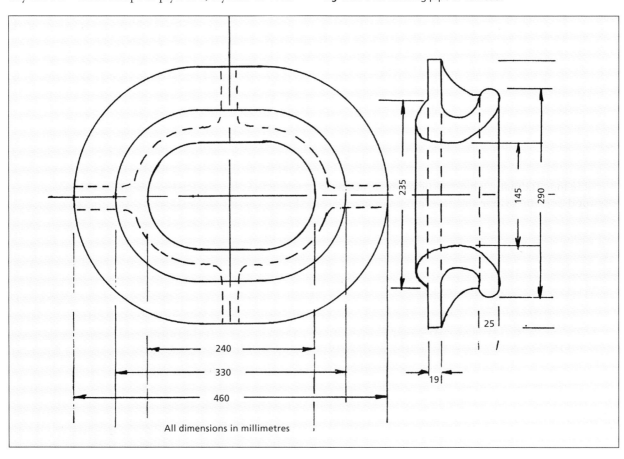

240

330

460

235

145

290

25

19

All dimensions in millimetres

on most ships including tugs also admit light and air to the engine room. In these cases, they are often sited immediately above the engine(s) and, in the case of the steam driven tug, almost always have the top covers wide open to the atmosphere to speed the egress of heat. In some cases, small fixed-pattern skylights can be found set into the foredeck, fixed to prevent any possibility of water entering and designed to admit light to the a cabin. These small skylights have very strong glass and are designed to allow work to be carried on above them. The skylights fitted

Hydraulic windlass on foredeck of tug model. Photo by Model Slipway.

above the engine room and/or boiler room of the ship will not only have large areas of glass in frames that can be raised, but will also usually have steel bars to protect the glass from breakage. Although most skylights are usually fully glazed, some are made of steel and have port lights let into them as can be seen in some of the deck and full vessel photographs.

Model skylights are fairly easy to construct being little more than rectangular boxes with sloping tops running longitudinally. They can be made from thin plywood or from styrene sheet, with the sloping tops being made up of transparent sections. Where necessary, sections of the tops (windows) can be shown in the open position and it is always intriguing to be able to see the steam engine or the drive equipment through the glazing. Protective bars can and either painted or polished – the latter recalling some of the earlier tugs with protective brass bars that were always kept highly polished.

Funnels and masts

All tugs have funnels of one kind or another. The funnels on steam tugs differ from those of motor ships and so the modeller needs to know the differences if the model is to depict accurately a real vessel.

Steam tug funnels can be round, oval or ovoid and also streamlined – but all serve the same purpose. They all have an inner flue through which the exhaust gases from the boiler(s) are discharged to atmosphere. The outer funnel assists insulation of the inner funnel and ensures that the hot gases remain at high temperature until they reach the air. All flue gases from furnaces need to be kept as hot as is practical in order to prevent them condensing on the steel of the flues, such condensation being acidic and capable of causing serious corrosion. The outer funnel will, of course, remain cool enough to allow decorative finishes to be applied. The modeller who builds incorporating a model steam plant will use the outer funnel to cover the chimney of the model boiler and thus replicate the arrangement of the full-size tug.

Motor-driven tugs have funnels of very many different shapes but like a steam-powered vessel, these funnels also serve to exhaust the hot gases from the oil-fuelled engines. Frequently, they also contain the silencers needed to reduce engine noise and provide the back pressure necessary to allow the engine to perform correctly. Twin-engine tugs usually have twin funnels, usually sited on either side of the superstructure. Most diesel tugs will have the funnel capped with short stubs of exhaust pipes protruding above the capping. Such is the diversity of the funnels of the modern tug that only one or two

Fig 13.11: Examples of tow hooks.

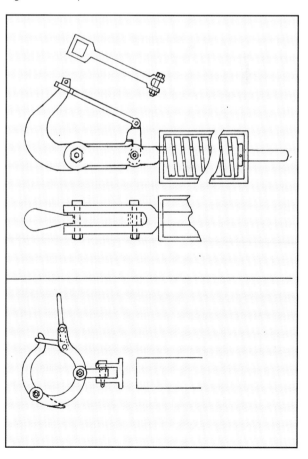

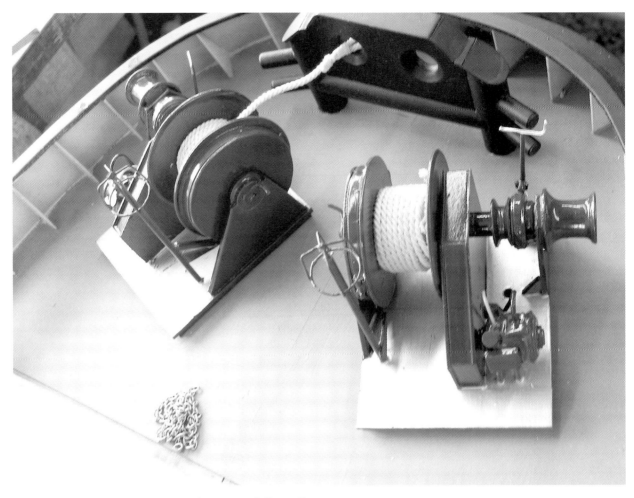

Twin winches on the foredeck of the model tug 'AYTON CROSS'.

are illustrated in these pages and the tug modeller will need to research his chosen vessel carefully to ensure accuracy.

All tugs, whether steam or motor driven, generally have a siren mounted on the fore side of the funnel, with many have access ladders so that the siren or whistle can be serviced. A steam tug will almost certainly have two pipes running up the funnel – one to feed steam to the siren or whistle and the other leading from the safety valve on the boiler to release escaping steam safely to the atmosphere. Some of the funnels on a diesel tug also carry its stern-facing navigation lights. On steam tugs, some funnels were rigged with wire guy ropes incorporating tensioners that were fixed to the decks. Details like these will be evident in photographs of full-size vessel selected for modelling.

Masts were originally fitted to ships for the purpose of carrying sails. Indeed, the very early steam tugs often continued to carry sails of one kind or another. However masts outlived the sail era as they also fulfil a useful function on more modern vessels.

Today the mast carries radio aerials, radar units and navigation lights. Sometimes, masts also have blocks and lifting tackle for handling small boats or provisions. They also carry flags and ensigns that will depict the country of registration or origin of the tug, the identity of its owners or – as a matter of courtesy – the flag of the country being visited. In short the

mast has a multiplicity of uses.

Most tugs will carry but a single mast, often on top of the wheelhouse or superstructure, or on the forward side of the funnel. This mast will certainly carry the forward-facing navigation lights, possibly the radar units and probably some aerials for the radio. (Details of the navigation lights and other lights for the tug will be found later in this chapter). On most tugs, there will be smaller masts, usually on the top of the bridge, that carry other lights associated with towing duties (also described later).

Many steam-driven tugs carried two masts. As a rule, these were located with one at each end of the superstructure, with the radio aerials slung between them. They also carried navigation lamps and were rigged to carry signal flags and ensigns, with the after mast usually mounted a small derrick that was used most often for handling the workboat. Some of the types of masts to be found on a tug can be seen in some of the photographs.

There are a number of methods of making the mast for a model tug, the simplest being to shape it from a length of suitable timber dowel that is readily available from most model shops in a range of diameters. Almost all masts taper from base to truck

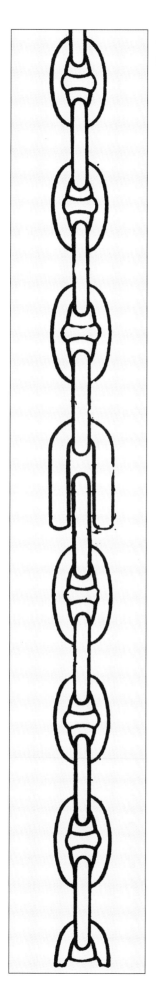

Fig 13.14: Drawing of standard pattern anchor cable

(top), so the dowel will need to be planed or sanded to conform to the required shape, tapering in straight run and not curved from base to truck. The easiest way to hold the dowel for tapering is to fit it into a groove cut into a piece of hardwood and in which the dowel can be slowly revolved while it is being progressively sanded or planed. A length of dowel that is planed to a taper will certainly need to be finished by sanding.

Steel masts can be made in model form using thin wall brass tube, also available from good model shops. Such tube comes in varying diameters that allow each size to slide neatly into the larger one. It is thus possible to produce a tapered mast by slotting the necessary sizes of tube into one another, until the required length is finally obtained. Making the mast in this way allows the modeller to fit working navigation lights easily, as the tube itself can form the return path for the current feeding each lamp (see 12.4 page 41).

Almost all masts will have specific fittings. Most comprise bands fitted round the mast and either clamped by bolts and nuts, pegged in a number of places, or welded into place. Near the truck, the band will usually carry a bracket for the radio aerial – although the more modern tug will rely on whip aerials (rods). There will also be brackets to carry the navigation lights or pulleys to allow the navigation lights to be lowered and raised for servicing, in the case of the earlier tugs. With wooden masts, the bands can be made easily from thin card glued in place and painted black. Then, small eyebolt can be fitted through such bands into pre-drilled holes and secured with 'Superglue'. Eyebolts can be used to hold blocks in place or to secure stays and shrouds for the mast support.

Bands for metal masts can similarly be made from card but need to be secured with superglue for security, but they can also be made from thin brass strip soldered in place. Many tug kit makers will supply mast bands cast in white metal or in hard plastic and which can be secured in place with 'Superglue' or one of the two part epoxy resins.

Working lights for masts, etc.

There is something special about a model tug or other vessel sailing in the dusk with a full set of correctly fitted lights shining brightly. The fitting of working lights is not difficult, although the job does need care. A tug carries a veritable Christmas tree of lights, on or near the fore mast, and the modeller needs to be fully aware of the correct location and colour of such lights.

A basic navigation light set comprises two bright white lights facing forward, usually on the fore mast In full size practice, these are set about 2 metres apart, with one white light facing the stern (usually on the aft rail of the superstructure), another, red light facing forward (in a boxed casing on the port side of the bridge or similar high point) and a similar forward-facing green light on the starboard side. These are the lights needed in order to comply with international rules for navigation after dark; but a tug will carry an additional number of lights of general, all-round illumination, These are generally in white, green and red, arranged in internationally agreed patterns to indicate what work the tug is doing. The light arrangements of lights are shown in the diagrams accompanying Appendix 5.

Classification Society rules demand that electrically-operated navigation lights must be capable of being illuminated at all times. With earlier vessels, this meant that at each location, an electric lamp would also have above it an oil lamp for use should the generator fail. More modern vessels carry twin electric lamps at each location, one set operating from the main generator and the second connected to a battery system that is kept fully charged for emergency use.

Because of all this, the model tug builder needs to be certain of the period of the tug being built in order to ensure the correct lights are fitted. Most usually, power for a model lighting system comes from the main drive battery, i.e. 6 or 12 volts DC, Whilst this is perfectly satisfactory, many of the very small light bulbs that need to be fitted will be very, very difficult to replace should they fail. Consequently, it is advisable to fit bulbs needing a higher current than that available as such light bulbs will still provide a bright light but will be less prone to failure due to the lower current supply. For example, a 6-volt lamp fed from a 4-volt supply will last a long time. So, it is probably sensible to fit a separate battery solely to supply the lighting system.

As mentioned above, lights on a metal mast can use the mast itself as the return current source as illustrated in Appendix 5. However, timber mast lights need to have their cables run in a groove in the mast in order to conceal them or run up the aft side of the mast very carefully and glued in place to simulate electrical conduit. The lights fitted on the superstructure are easier to illuminate than those on a mast; but the modeller needs to build the superstructure with the lighting in mind, so that the wires can be concealed within the unit.

Many model kit manufacturers include navigation lights within their range of fittings and do so in different scales. Some will be plain castings unsuitable for illumination, but others are suitable for carrying the small lamps used for lighting. Some modellers advocate the use of LED lamps (light-emitting diodes) for model lighting. Whilst these appear to be almost indestructible, they do need to be installed with correct polarity and require small resistors within their circuitry.

The most commonly used model lamps are very small and known as 'grain of wheat' or 'grain of rice' bulbs – the former being larger than the 'rice'. They are available in white, green, red, blue and yellow colours and suitable for 3-, 6-, 9- and 12-volt supplies. The choice of which to use is open to the modeller; and the author has fitted all of the types listed with complete success. However, in this context and from experience, it should be noted that handling, soldering and positioning of small lamps is a delicate task.

Radar equipment, etc.

Radar units are frequently installed on purpose-made platforms that are attached to the mast. A tug will usually have two revolving scanners on separate platforms, mounted one above the other, often above the wheelhouse or immediately forward of it.

Smaller tugs might also have a smaller scanner that is concealed inside a container that looks not unlike a large, flat biscuit tin. This is an easier type to model than the revolving scanners; but both can be formed from scrap pieces of wood or plastic that has been suitably shaped and glued in place.

Real radar scanners revolve fairly slowly in service and some modellers like to make their scanner operate in a like manner. This necessitates using small, geared motors and fine flexible shafts for the purpose. As the speed of the scanner does not vary, there is no need for a speed control unit.

Other items found on the top of the bridge or wheelhouse will often include a direction finding loop - usually seen only on tugs before 1950 – and a searchlight or two. Model searchlights made to precise scales can be found in the ranges of fittings from the major model kit manufacturers, some inclusive of lamp and with the facility of being illuminated.

Almost all tugs will carry a binnacle on the top of the wheelhouse and some will also have an engine room telegraph unit. The binnacle is a requirement of those Classification Societies that specify a second compass system for use in the event of the modern electronic wheelhouse units failing from lack of power, etc. The modern tug will certainly mount a binnacle, but engine room telegraphs are not now – control of engines being generally from the wheelhouse under the hand of the tug master.

Many tugs today also carry one or more fire monitors on top of the bridge or wheelhouse. Some even have a special tower built above the bridge to carry such fire fighting equipment. A typical fire monitor is illustrated in the diagram (Fig. 13/13) and model versions can often be bought from the specialist model shops and mail order outlets. Some can even be fitted to operate from a pump located within the hull. When running and drawing water from the lake or pond, they make for an attractive feature.

Guard rails, ladders, etc.

Little is written on the subject of guardrails, yet virtually all tugs will have some form of guard rail installed for the safety of the working personnel.

Stanchions of the cast ball pattern can be bought from many model outlets and in many sizes. From these it is possible to make suitable guard rails using appropriately sized brass or piano wire. The more modern, flat bar pattern stanchions etched in fine brass or nickel plate can also be from a few suppliers; these too need brass or similar wire to complete their construction.

This is probably the place to state that the most common fault or point of criticism to found on almost all tug models is related to the guard rails. All such rails should always have atop rail that is 1.5–2 times greater in diameter that the lower rails; but commercially available, ball pattern stanchions or flat bar pattern stanchions rarely cater for this requirement. However, with the flat bar pattern, the problem can easily be rectified by cutting off the top of the stanchion through the centre of the top hole and soldering larger diameter wire into the resulting dimple. In the case of the ball pattern stanchion, the answer is to drill out the top hole to accept larger wire – if at all possible. Guard rails that are poorly made and installed are very conspicuous on an otherwise fine model. Thus, their modelling and fitting really do demand careful attention.

Ladders and companionways are found on all vessels including tugs. As a result, ladders are included among many of the kit maker's fittings – usually cast in white metal, formed in hard plastic or etched in fine brass. All three types have their place on the model. Of course, depending upon scale, they can also be made by drilling lengths of fine timber strips at regular intervals. Then, using appropriately sized wire, combining the side strips and wire to make the required ladder. But it can be a fairly onerous task demanding great accuracy.

Companionways can be found in the model ship shop just as readily as ladders. Again, they tend to be cast in white metal, formed in hard plastic or etched in brass, etc. and come in a variety of scales. They too can be made by the modeller, using fine timber or thin styrene sheet or strip with treads of the same material. However, they are much more complex and difficult to make than are ladders. The side strips need to be accurately grooved to accept the treads and the modeller should remember that a full size companion has risers of seven inches and treads of nine inches wide (180 mm high and 230 mm wide), so that the model needs to be built to these scale sizes.

Ladders affixed to masts are often simply steel bars that have been bent and welded in place, rather than being purpose-built ladders fixed to the mast with brackets. Almost all mast ladders also have safety loops at intervals of one metre (just over 3 ft) to provide extra safety the person climbing the ladder in adverse conditions extra safety. One or two model manufacturers do make ladders with safety loops in certain scales and so it is worth the tug modeller searching out for such accessories – even if only to

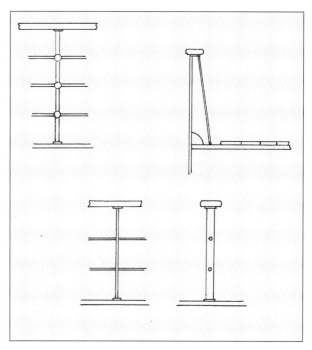

Fig 13.12: Examples of guard rails and bulwark tops

avoid the somewhat exacting task of making them in the workshop. Soft brass wire is easily formed into loops and winding the wire closely as a number of turns round a rod of suitable diameter will provide a spring that can then be cut with shears - and immediately one has a number of wire circles from which to make the ladder loops.

Auxiliary systems

By now, the reader will probably have noticed that no mention has been made of making or installing additional working features for a model tug. Adding an element of sound, modelling actual working winches and windlass, etc. are subjects that have been covered many times in the model press.

Guard rail detail round bridge unit of vessel

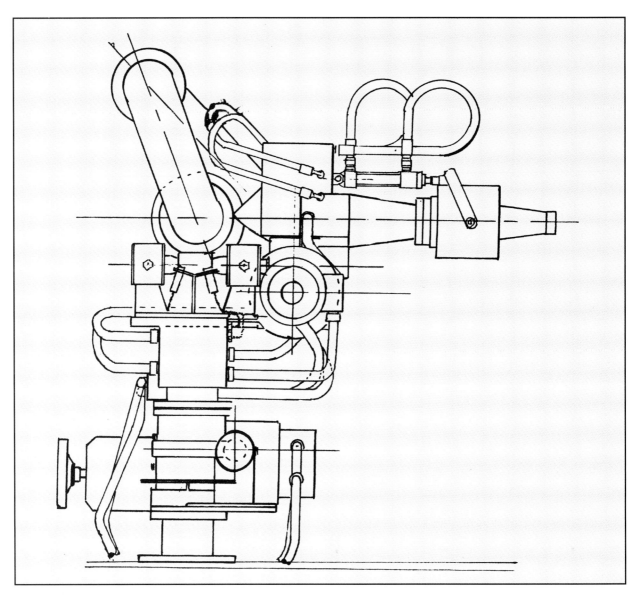

Fig 13.13 Arrangement of fire monitor.

A number of manufacturers make and offer for sale systems that can simulate the sound of the ship's engines and have this even arranged to vary in sympathy with the speed of the drive equipment. Horns and sirens are also available for installing in the model tug hull. These specialist items, being readily purchased and then fitted to suit individual requirements will definitely enhance the model, particularly if well installed and operated sensibly.

That is fine when it comes to sound, but having working winches, windlasses and capstans is generally down to the ingenuity of the model builder. Few examples are available in either kit or ready-built forms and so have to be constructed by the modeller.

This is usually achieved using parts taken from static model kits of the chosen unit. Some examples made in this way have been known to operate very well, and a working towing winch is a decided advantage to the modeller who enjoys towing with the tug. Nevertheless, and whilst well worth a mention, the specialist nature of such items rather debars any attempt here to expand upon them – especially as there are sources of information and data in most model ship magazines and in a number of books have been written on the subject.

Chapter 14

Painting and Finishing

It is a sad but true observation that many otherwise well-built models are spoiled by the quality and application of their paint and varnish. Good paintwork can only be obtained by careful preparation beforehand. The surfaces to which the paint is to be applied must be well prepared and free from blemishes. Marks left by tools and sanding will show clearly through the layers of paint and completely mar the surface. Even the smallest fitting needs to be carefully examined and prepared soundly for the application of paint. When the surface has been made good and the paint has been applied, then it needs the protection of two or three coats of good quality varnish. Although the paint itself may well provide a good finish, matt or satin paints will show finger marks of handling if not protected by varnish. If not gloss, then and a matt or satin varnish will provide the necessary protection.

During the course of building the model, it will be obvious that some surfaces need to be painted and varnished before being fitted and then become difficult to reach. The sensible and experienced good modeller will identify these places and provide the required treatments before proceeding further. Small fittings that also need to be painted can be treated at any time during the construction, e.g. when waiting for glue or other treatment to dry or cure. This course of action will also save time when the time comes for the pieces to be attached to the model.

Just as good tools are needed to effect good quality work, so are good brushes needed for producing a fine paint finish. High-grade, small artists brushes are a sound investment, watercolour brushes of

Neatly painted model of the tug 'RATHGARTH'.

Carefully laid planked deck – not on a tug but to show method.

Left: Further deck planking details.

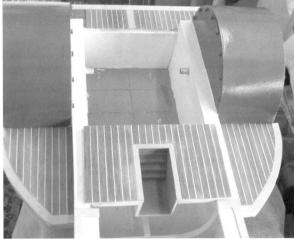

sable being the very best, though most expensive. In addition, just as good tools need to be maintained in top condition, so good brushes need similar attention. They should be cleaned as soon as work of the moment is completed. Any excess paint should be squeezed carefully from the bristles and the brush should be washed in the thinners appropriate to the type of paint being used.

Successive washes in two or three pots of thinners is the minimum treatment recommended, after which the brush should be lightly dried on a soft cloth or tissue, placed head up in a jar and left to dry completely. Wherever possible, it is wise to assign a brush to a specific colour; but where the brushes may be used for different colours, thorough cleaning is essential.

There a number of brush-cleaning products on the market and most are very useful. (For example, Squires – see Appendix 2 – have such products

available that are both very effective.) Brushes that have become stiff with paint that has built up in the heel of the bristles can be restored by soaking the brush in cellulose thinners for a short period of time and then working loose the hardened paint residue. Two or more successive soakings will usually restore any brush, which should be washed in warm water and detergent before being gently rinsed. It is worth repeating: good brushes need care and, if at all possible, should never be left to go hard.

Today, the majority of modellers will have recourse to the spray cans of colours and primers, etc. available from many stores and model shops. These sprays come in a variety of materials, with cellulose, enamel and acrylic being the most common (although cellulose is now becoming rare). In the author's opinion, the best in quality versus price are the cans of acrylic spray paints available throughout the U.K. from Halfords stores. These cans have fine nozzles, consistent colours on a can-to-can basis, and will be completely empty of paint before the propellant is dispersed.

Wherever possible, cellulose-based paints should be avoided. When sprayed over an enamel or acrylic, primer or undercoat, cellulose will attack the previous coating so badly that the whole model will have to be stripped and re-painted. In fact, before treating a good model or hull, all modellers would be wise to check the paints they are considering by spraying a test piece. The same rules apply to the type of varnish being used, as it should also be tested before applying

Model of stern paddle wheeler – medal winning model – to illustrate painting quality.

to the finished paint surface. Get it wrong and many hours may be needed to rectify such a fault and obtain a satisfactory result. The point is made deliberately as there have been occasions when the author has had to effect serious restoration when the varnish being used has adversely affected the paint finish.

In preference to the artists brush, many modellers will use an airbrush and it is an excellent method of applying the preferred colour. Whether the airbrush is driven from a can of propellant or from an air compressor makes little difference, although if an airbrush is to be used a great deal, then a compressor of reasonable cost will prove the less expensive option in the long run. As with normal brushes, an airbrush and its containers need to be cleaned regularly after each colour is used; and, again, suitable cleaning fluid has to be used according to the type of paint in use. Specially made cleaning outfits can be purchased from mail order outlets such as Squires (Appendix 2).

There are a number of manufacturers worldwide who specialise in producing paint for the model maker. Each company has a range of colours in matt, satin and gloss finishes – and there is usually a clear varnish in the same finishes. Almost all produce paints with an oil base and an acrylic base. Paints produced by an individual maker are usually compatible one with another, but not all paints from one maker will match or be intermixable with those of another. Some paints will attack styrene and ABS plastics so that testing the product before using it is always a good idea.

Many manufacturers have both enamel and acrylic paints in their range. Enamels are spirit-based paints that can be mixed together in order to produce differing shades, although the same maker's brand of thinner must be used to dilute them. In fact, although some paints will work with turpentine substitute or white spirit as a dilutant, the maker's own thinner is generally the best choice. In contrast, most acrylic paints are water-based and can be thinned with clean, clear water, even though the paint is both waterproof and hard when dry. Note, however, that acrylics cannot be intermixed with enamels.

Both acrylics and enamels can, when suitably diluted, be used in an airbrush – separately, of course. Both types usually require special thinners when used in this way and the modeller needs to check this before committing the paint to the brush.

Painting the hull

The first part of a model tug usually to be painted is the hull. Once the propeller shaft(s), bilge keels, rudder and post, etc. have been fitted in place, the whole surface of the hull should be examined very carefully. All remaining imperfections should be made good before any paint is applied.

Initially, a wooden hull is best prepared by treating it with two or three coats of 'spray filler'. This is a yellow-coloured compound available in spray cans from most car accessory dealers. Alternatively, use or two or three coats of sanding sealer, as this will fill any small spaces in the wood grain and smooth out any very small blemishes. Each coating of the filler should be allowed to dry thoroughly for at least four hours before being rubbed down lightly with a 400- or

600-grit abrasive paper used on a block. Once sanded, the final coat should be allowed at least 24 hours to harden fully before any further paint is applied. At no time should any timber hull should be rubbed down with wet abrasive paper, as the water will certainly raise the grain of the timber - and the raised grain will take considerable time to dry before it can be sanded to the fine surface needed to proceed. In contrast, dry the abrasives cut through to the timber.

A GRP hull should be washed thoroughly with warm water and detergent in order to remove any traces of the release agent that has been used during manufacture. The hull should then be rubbed all over with 400-grit abrasive paper that will provide a 'key' for the paint. It should then be rinsed with clean water and laid aside to dry in a warm atmosphere. For the best results, two or three coats of a quality primer should be applied – by either brush or by spray – and each coating lightly rubbed down with 400- or 600-grit abrasive paper on a block. The hull will then need at least overnight drying in a dry warm place so that the primer is able to cure and before any other paints are applied. Having been thus treated, the hull should not be handled any more than is absolutely necessary; hands are naturally greasy and grease will prevent paint from adhering. A light rub-over with methylated spirit will remove any grease and leave the hull ready for the paint.

Having prepared the hull, either of timber or GRP, it can now be painted in its final colours. Most ships hulls are treated below the waterline with red oxide anti-fouling paint. So, with a model, if whole hull is sprayed with red oxide colour, then the bottom will not need further treatment except for varnishing. If, however, the upper part of the hull is white or a very light colour, then the hull should be sprayed all over with a light gray or white primer first. In the latter case, the hull will need to be lined off at the waterline for the bottom of the hull to be sprayed the colour of red oxide.

In either of the above cases, the waterline is best marked on the hull using a sharp soft pencil clamped to a block or to square - as illustrated in the photograph * that can be drawn around the hull, which itself must be firmly fixed to a flat surface and packed, in order to bring the waterline parallel to the flat surface. The hull can then be masked off at the drawn line using a fine, thin masking tape (such as that made by Tamiya) and sold in most model shops. The masking should follow the curvature of the hull and ensure that the paint will not leech through. Over this masking tape, attach clean dry paper over the hull but beneath or above the finely masked line. Two or three coats of the appropriate colour can then be applied, by either brush or by spray, each being carefully examined, rubbed down as necessary and allowed to dry for some hours before applying the next coat. In practice, it is not unusual for a hull to have more than three coats of the finish colour but all

should be thinned and applied evenly.

Finally, when completely painted and after name, port of registry and all other printed items have been applied, the hull should be given two coats of suitable varnish. For working models, it is wise to use a matt varnish, as any working tug rarely looks in any way glossy or shiny, even when seen close up. On the other hand, if the model is to be kept in a glass case solely for display purposes, then a satin-finish varnish is commended.

When using automotive spray paints, such as those supplied by Halfords and other car accessory dealers, be aware that they are designed to be baked hard in special oven once they have been applied fully. So, it is wise to place the model painted in this way in a warm, dry and preferably dust-free place and allow up to three weeks for the paint to cure correctly. This may not be quite so much of an idle time as it seems if the superstructure and other main parts of the model can be constructed while the hull is curing in this way.

Painting the superstructure, etc.

Applying the coats of paint needed for the superstructure, simply follow the procedure given for the hull – except that it is unlikely that any part will need to be masked off quite so carefully. The exception will be where the real tug being modelled (the prototype) has a superstructure painted in two different colours. Whatever, all of the small surfaces involved will best be treated using fine brushes or an airbrush.

When brush painting, the paint should be thinned to the consistency of single cream and applied quickly and with the broadest brush that will allow sensible coverage of the small areas. Do not go over the surface repeatedly. This will lead to brush strokes showing clearly, the removal of which, on small surfaces, is very difficult and time taking.

These points apply equally to the use of both enamel and acrylic paint. But beware when using acrylic paints, as they tend to dry very rapidly indeed. Aim always to achieve a thin but good coverage for each coat of paint; and allow adequate time between coats for the paint to dry fairly well. Remember too that, where a heavy coating is applied, the top may seem to be dry whilst beneath this top layer the paint may still be liquid. So, if abrasives are used too soon the whole coating will be damaged. The simple rule is that any modeller really needs to be very, very patient when applying paint to their model.

Use of an airbrush on the superstructure makes the task easier than using a normal brush for painting – but the airbrush also has its problems. This is where it will probably be necessary to apply some masking in order to avoid the sprayed paint from over-coating a small area. Where the area is very small, it is worth using a liquid masking compound that can be applied with a small brush. Once this liquid has dried, the

View of tug model 'AFON ALAW to show lettering, logo and finish.

Detail of bow of paddle steamer.

relevant part can be sprayed. Then, once painting is completed, the masking can be removed together with its paint by carefully picking it away with a fine blade. Liquid masking like this can also be used to cover clear glazing that has had to be fitted before the section can be painted. The masking will not damage clear glazing material and it can be bought in small bottles from most good model shops.

Where paint is to be applied to parts that have to revolve or oscillate, apply only thin coats and allow each coat to dry well. At the same time and at regular intervals, operate the movement so that the paint does not seal up the required action.

With small parts, it is often best to fix them to a scrap length of timber with double-sided adhesive tape and allow them to be spray- or brush-painted. Small parts like these are best first treated with a couple of thin coats of white primer. This will emphasise small details and allow the finish coatings to be applied with little problem. In addition, always allow ample time for the paint to dry before attaching them to the model in their appropriate positions.

As for the hull, superstructure and deck fittings, machinery, etc., they all need to be varnished and to

be allowed ample drying time. If necessary, fine detail can be enhanced by using satin varnish in selected places, while the whole is finished in matt.

Anchor cables (chains) are usually painted black; but some have sections painted white – so that the operator lowering or raising the anchor is able to calculate the distance the cable travels.

Painting rigging shrouds, aerials and similar fine wires is a delicate job. The decks and areas below and around the rigging, etc. need to be covered with scraps of clean paper to prevent splashes of paint

Above: Finished paintwork on model paddler.

Below: Model 'SHANKLIN' showing the effect of deck planking, painting etc.

Right: After deck of 'SHANKLIN' showing attention to detail.

marring finished surfaces. Also, painting wires invariably causes small drops of paint to be spread around. Decks that have been made with caulked planking should be sealed with fine matt varnish, they can be lightly sanded before repeating the varnish; but always remember how the caulking has been applied in order to avoid its black colouring from being picked up and spread when the deck is sanded. No working decks are ever shiny, so matt varnish is a must in this case.

Finishing

The general painting of hull and superstructure being complete, detail work is needed before one can say that the model is finished – that is, if any modeller can say that they are ever finished.

Thus, there remains the matter of all the words and lettering to be found on all ships. A ship's name needs to be applied, usually on either side of the bow and on the stern, together with the vessel's port of registry. In most cases, such lettering is in white. Those on the bow are of a reasonably large size whilst the stern name appears smaller and the port of registry even smaller.

Where the tug has a stern ramp and rollers, the name and port may be on both sides of the vessel, near the stern, or the name may be on one side of the stern ramp and the registry port on the other.

White lettering is available in many sizes and typefaces from a number of specialist suppliers (see Appendix 2). Some versions are supplied in a form where letters need to be carefully removed from a backing sheet and applied one at a time to the selected position on the model. To ensure that they are applied in a straight line and are evenly spaced, it is sensible to place a length of fine masking tape to delineate the line and aid the eye when applying the letters. The supplier B.E.C.C. provides many ranges of such letters and also provides depth marks for the bow and stern of the model tug, together with the Plimsoll line markings and lettering in a number of sizes.

Letters and numbers, signs and Plimsoll marks can also be bought in the form of waterslide transfers. However, waterslide transfers have a carrier film that will show up clearly on the hull if these transfers are applied to satin or matt surfaces. To make this backing film 'disappear', the area where the transfer is to be placed should first be given a coat of high gloss varnish and allowed to dry thoroughly before the transfer is applied. Once the applied transfer is dry, the area can be re-covered with satin or matt varnish and it will

seem as if the transfer's carrier film has been concealed.

When creating a model of a real vessel and wherever possible, the tug modeller should obtain photographs that show the lettering and signs appearing on the real vessel's hull. On the model, they will be quite small and so need very careful attention to obtain an authentic result. The effort is worthwhile, as their inclusion will enhance considerably the quality of the build. Some are shown in accompanying photographs for guidance.

The most modern practice is also to have the vessels running numbers, albeit in very small size and generally upon the stern below the port of registry. Some lettering can also be found on the funnels of some tugs and indicating the owners of the tug; and some tugs also have funnels painted in distinct colours with the owner's logo applied to the smoke stack(s).

All lettering and numbers should, of course, be varnished to ensure that it adheres firmly to the selected location; and it goes without saying that the area where the letters and numbers are to be applied should be clean, dry and free from grease and finger marks before letters are applied.

Some modellers attach ensigns and flags to their models. This is not a difficult task as fine cloth flags in a huge range of sizes can be bought from a number of makers. Some of these also produce replica 'House flags' depicting the owner of the vessel. Sensibly, all flags fitted to a model should be shown draped down more than spread wide – only in very high winds would an ensign spread wide. For a tug, the appropriate U.K. ensign – red, blue or white – would be flown from a jackstaff at or near the stern; the house flag would usually fly from the main mast; and there will rarely be other flags or pennants

Above: Finely painted and varnished model of 'MOORCOCK'
Photo courtesy of Ray Brigden.

Left: Superstructure for 'AYTON CROSS' to show effect of light
on two sections of equal colour – light cream showing yellow on
lower unit.

Below left: Superstructure of 'AYTON CROSS' to show paint
application.

Below: Wheel house for 'AYTON CROSS' showing careful use of
transparent styrene and subsequent painting.

Above right: Finished superstructure of 'AYTON CROSS' to show
detail.

Right: Beautifully finished and painted model by Model Slipway.

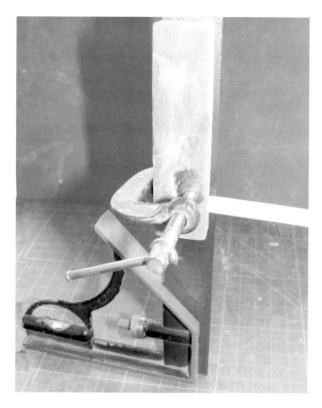

Lock and pencil attached to steel square to allow waterline to be drawn round the hull of a model tug.

obvious. The red ensign is the standard Merchant Marine indication a blue ensign indicates a vessel in Admiralty use but sailed with a merchant crew; and the white ensign being reserved for vessel carrying and under the command of Royal Navy personnel. If a modeller wishes to include flags, then he/she will be wise to ensure that only the correct units are flown.

Finally, the modeller will have noticed that all tugs have some form of protection all around or almost completely around the hull. In most cases, this protection is in the form of old tyres, drilled to accept chains, or wire rope to permit them to be hung from the bulwarks. Some vessels have protection in the form of large rope, whilst others – particularly those tugs used for ship handling in confined waters – have large rubber covered beams affixed to their bows and round the stern. Almost all of these protective items can be found within the stocks of the good model ship shop or mail order outlet. They should be selected with care to ensure that they are of the correct scale size. They can easily be attached to the model with cord or fine chain, or with an appropriate adhesive.

Artificial wear and tear

No one judging models, either at a qualifying event or at a national final, will expect to find models of any type of ship in pristine condition. Most often, working vessels are best displayed in their 'working clothes' that show some degree of wear and tear. However,

applying artificial signs of weathering and distress to a model needs particular care. It is all too easy to slap on degrees of rusting to those places on a model where the modeller thinks rust will show, etc. Rather, weathering should be applied with reference to as many photographs as possible and should be minimal in order to obtain the best effect. Whenever there are any doubts regarding the locations of rusting and wear, the modeller is well advised to leave well alone until they have searched seriously into the problem.

The amount of wear and damage to a ship will vary greatly and be related very much to its area of duty. For example, a stern trawler newly arriving in port after a voyage of eight to ten weeks in Arctic waters will show evidence of a great deal of serious wear on the hull from ice and salt water in such latitudes. Contrastingly, a tug running only in the confines of the river and docks in a European port will remain reasonably clean over the same period of time.

Consideration should also be given to the ownership of the actual vessel that is modelled. Some ship owners will insist that their vessels are kept in a high degree of cleanliness and all ships hulls and superstructures remain well painted and sound – while others are not as fussy and look first to the cost of maintaining a ship in a fine condition. This variation means that some ships can look shabby when others do not. In the case of tugs, it is fair to say that those owned by their masters will usually look better than those owned and run by a conglomerate. Overall though, few tugs today are in the hands of their owners, with most being run by one of the large tug companies – whose tugs will vary from small harbour vessels to large, long-distance and salvage tugs that are all usually kept in fine condition. Most signs of wear are likely to be evident on the protective equipment around the sides, bow and stern of the tug, and to distress such parts of a tug model is far from a simple matter.

When entering a competition, especially where the model will be judged on a table by, a team of (usually) two or three qualified judges they will seek to assess the quality of the mode. In so doing, they will follow accepted route and set of criteria that involves awarding points for various aspects of the build. In a competition that is well organised, no model will be judged against another; each will be judged upon its own merits and points will only be deducted where such subtraction is agreed by full judging team.

In the type of competition where the purpose is to determine the abilities of the model tug master or team of tugs, how the tug is displayed becomes less important to the judges. However, one very valid point in most sailing competitions is how the model is sailed and the speed at which it is run. Running a model around a regatta course at more than scale speed will certainly lose the master some points. All too often, one sees tugs running at such high speed that looks as if they were in full-size, high-speed, round coast races. The good tug master will avoid such excess and find or assess the sensible speed at which the model should run, both when running free and when under towing conditions. As an indication, most full size tugs will, and can, run at speeds up to 15 knots – sometimes more. When 'translated' into scale speed on the local lake, this is quite slow. So, whilst it is always advantageous and quite pleasing to be able to run fast – e.g. to get out of trouble – never do so when under the scrutiny of the judge.

Most model ship judges are well qualified to assess the worth of the models that they assess. They will usually have had to take instruction and to pass through various tests to achieve their accreditation. A good tug master will never question the validity of the judging

at the time. Yet, there is nothing wrong in asking later about why or where the model lost points. All good judges will be happy to provide such information if approached after judging has taken place – but never during the judging time. Knowledge acquired in this way can then be used later to rectify any faults.

For many ship modellers, of tugs or any other type, the competitive spirit is not so evident or important and they enjoy simply building and sailing their models, either alone or in the company of friends. Some even prefer to build models purely for display purposes. Of whichever kind, all modellers seek to gain pleasure from their efforts – and for man, modelling a tug is certainly one way of doing so.

Sailing and Competition

Obviously, the sensible modeller will have tested the installation of drive equipment and radio during the building of the model or when it nears completion.

Once the painting and lettering, varnishing, etc., has been completed, then basin trials should be carried out. Usually, these first trials are generally carried out in the domestic bath or garden pond – depending upon permission for such areas having been obtained.

Invariably, one will find that the model will sail high in the water and that ballast will be needed to bring the tug down to the drawn line. The heavy, sealed lead-acid batteries will, without doubt, assist with this but often-additional ballast will be needed. Possibly the best method of adding weight is to use small pieces of lead sheet. The type used for flashing roofs is ideal and it is possible to buy pieces of small used pieces or off-cuts from a local jobbing builder. They can then be cut into rectangles, cleaned,

flattened and kept in stock for use as ballast.

In use, these small pieces of lead sheet should be placed carefully upon the floating model in order to determine how much weight is needed and approximately where it should be placed. The model can be taken back to the workbench and the ballast fitted carefully inside the hull at the identified locations. A repeated floating in the test tank will confirm if the ballast has been correctly installed, whereupon it can then be secured within the model to ensure that it cannot move.

The ballast should be installed so that the model is floating on an even keel. It is important to ensure that it is not low at the bow, a little low at the stern being better, for no ship should ever be allowed to sail

Lake laid out with hazards for steering course, towing competition etc.

bow down. In the real world, the first officer would be severely reprimanded if he allowed such a thing to occur.

It is also particularly important that ballast be secured firmly as shifting ballast can seriously interfere with the balance of the model, to the extent that it could even capsize. However, it is not always necessary to fit the ballast over the keel of the model. Weight very low down can make a model stiff in the water so that it does not roll slowly and realistically. Instead, thin sheet lead ballast can be fitted evenly up both sides of the model. Conversely, of course, a tender model that has a tendency to capsize will need weight very low in the hull to counteract the tendency.

Having successfully applied the ballast and ensured that the model is ready for its first trials, the modeller should next test the radio equipment and for this the services of an assistant are needed. The model should be taken out of doors and placed upon a wall, bench or other safe mounting. The radio equipment

should be switched on and the assistant should take the transmitter away from the model and operate the sticks at selected distances. A radio system that has been correctly installed should effectively control the model when the transmitter is operated at least 30 m (about 100 feet) or more away. If this fails, then the position and run of the receiver aerial should be examined – and, if necessary, re-located within the model until the signal operates the model. This type of test is really very wise before any model is taken to the water for its first trials.

The author has always tried to test run his models at a time when the local club water is sparsely occupied. Untested models can sometime be problematic and when there are a lot of models on the water, a test run can prove awkward. Running the tug forwards and backwards at varying speeds will allow the modeller to become accustomed to the positions of the sticks on the transmitter and their relation to the model. Turning circles in both clockwise and anticlockwise directions will allow you to find the diameter of the turning circles – clockwise can be quite different to anticlockwise, particularly when running a single-screw model. Rapid stops to avoid problems can be achieved by use of reverse thrust; but the tug master needs to know that such rapid and immediate reverse running can cause the model to swing one way or another.

In these ways, the good model tug master will

Above left: Model ships in use on a course used for steering and other competitions.

Below left: Further competition course details.

Below: More course details.

Overall view of course for National Finals at Balne Moor in September 2008.

learn the behaviour of the vessel under all possible conditions before attempting to carry out any towing. If the tug has a ramp at the stern, then running astern at more than dead slow speed can force water up the ramp and over the model's decks. This can be dangerous, as flooding can enter the hull and cause problems with radio and electrical equipment. Initially, a test over perhaps 15 to 30 minutes is a good idea, after which the model can be lifted from the water and examined carefully. Further and lengthier sailings can then be tried.

Once the first trial is completed, the model tug should be examined very carefully. Motors should be checked for heat – a motor running hot is not a good sign and reasons for overheating should be investigated and rectified as soon as is possible and before the model is again run. Batteries, too, should be cool as a battery overheating is also indicative of fault. Simple checks – such as ensuring that the propeller shaft(s) is properly lubricated and the propeller(s) is secure – should be automatic. Examination of the inside of the hull for signs of water ingress should be made after each outing and any source of such water entering the hull needs to be found and repaired. Finally, the security of internal items such as batteries, radio receiver and battery pack, electronic speed control units, etc. is important

and regular checking is wise. Overall, regular sailing will allow the tug master to become more proficient, and practice makes perfect.

The good tug master will always have a small tool kit ready to take to the water, the pack containing those small tools that are often needed to make minor adjustments at the water side. A spare set of fully charged batteries are also very useful and will save many problems if the originally installed units fail.

Joining a model boat club is always a wise course of action for the ship modeller. Such a club will provide access to controlled water for sailing and to the company of like-minded individuals – as well as offer a place where modelling is discussed, where information is exchanged and help provided. Most model boat clubs are friendly places and most modellers enjoy the slightly competitive air of sailing in company – and the beginner will usually get a great deal of help and friendly advice.

Usually, membership of a reputable model boat club also carries with it insurance of the third party pattern, thereby safeguarding the modeller in the event of their model causing an accident that involves

The table full of trophies awaiting presentation at the M.P.B.A. National Finals at Balne Moor 2008.

private property or a member of the public. At some venues and/or when a modeller may not be a member of a model boat club, the club officials may require proof of insurance before the modeller will be allowed to sail. Thus, it should be noted that sailing on any other than privately owned lakes or ponds, the modeller will need third party insurance. The question of insurance is especially important when steam driven models are involved.

At regular intervals, the average model boat club members will lay out a course on the lake and hold a regatta, where the members will sail their models round the course avoiding the hazards and gaining points for accurate navigation. Such events are good fun, being not always seriously intended as a competitive event, but for the entertainment of the membership.

Competitive events will also form part of the club's activities when other clubs attend and compete with each other. Among these will be times when towing large, unpowered models round the laid-out course is part of the competition. Tug towing has become very popular over the years and many tug modellers have

become proficient in the handling their tugs when towing large models around the lake.

Some modellers, of course, prefer to sail their models purely for their own pleasure; and some build their model tugs purely for display within glass cases. But all will find that membership of a model boat club has something to offer and where they can also offer back something from their own experiences.

Tug towing competitions

Of course, working tugs are designed to handle larger vessels and to tow barges and ships from one place to another. Thus, these are all activities and duties can and are replicated with most model tugs. However, towing with the model tug is not quite so easy as one might expect. A fair degree of skill must be developed in order to be able to successfully tow a large model around a course that has been designed to resemble in miniature that of moving up a river or similar area of water. All of that – and then to berth the tow accurately. This is where the security of the tow hook or winch becomes important and the towing point on the model should not be fitted to any part of the model that is detachable for access. A secure point should be braced from keel and sides of the hull, and fixed carefully and firmly so that the strain of the tow rope is as evenly distributed over the whole model rather than being concentrated on one small point.

First of all, let us consider towing a single, large barge or ship with only one's own tug. Single tug towing like this is by far the most difficult of the towing jobs. Even starting the tow can be problematic, as simple inertia often requires quite some power to start the tow moving. Then, once moving, stopping is also very difficult.

Whilst it is all too easy to rope up to the tow, use a short line and draw the tow round a simple course, it is also all too easy when stopping for the tow to overrun the tug and cause serious problems. Equally, it is very easy too to turn the tug until it is side-on to the tow, when all sorts of problems can occur. Slow and steady is the watchword for single tug towing, with care needed to slow the tow down at the right time and to turn within set confines.

The model tug master will need to practice single tug towing to gain the necessary experience and will benefit from the assistance of a more experienced tug master able to correct mistakes and assist the modeller with good advice. A good bridle is also necessary, as it will assist the turning of the tow. In real life, single tug towing relates more to towing over long distances than it does to ship handling in confined waters.

Some tugs are designed to push rather than to pull and so have a substantial structure at the bow to aid this function. In general, the push tug will rope closely to the stern of the barge, or ship, so that the two become, in effect, a single ship driven from the stern. Twin barges or multiples of barges may be roped together so that a single tug can push the combination accurately. As far as can be ascertained (and as mentioned near the front of this book), this method of handling barges or similar vessels is prevalent in the U.S.A., but very much less so the U.K. In fact, at the time of writing, there do not appear to be any model competitions for this method of ship handling.

Ship handling using two tugs is very much the practice in many harbours, estuaries and rivers, where the modeller will see such work actually being carried out. In general, the lead tug ropes to the bow of the tow and carries out the majority of the actual towing. The second tug ropes to the stern of the tow and performs most of the steering and braking. But this is not quite as simple as it sounds.

The tows used in most model towing competitions are about six feet long (2 metres) and ballasted to a fair weight. So it is not easy to make it move from rest and requires a fair degree of power from the leading tug. Conversely, once moving, it is difficult to halt or slow down. Thus, handling such a large model and drawing it through narrow gates and canals on a steering course requires a great deal of care and agreement between the leading tug's master and that of the stern tug. Most of the model tug masters who are successful at regattas are those who have spent a fair degree of time working together and practicing the art of tug handling.

It should be noted that the model tug used for towing in the aforementioned paragraphs needs to be outfitted with drive gear that will provide the necessary power to start the tow smoothly and to keep it moving. This does not mean that the tug must be a large tug, but rather that it is fitted to give a good bollard pull.

Towing with a team of three tugs is only slightly different to that of towing with two. Tugs one and two will rope up to the bow and stern of the tow, and the third will roam free to assist by pushing the tow from one side or the other. In so doing it will be obvious that tug number three needs to have a heavily protected bow. Again, practice is needed for the team to become a proficient and coordinated team.

Among fellow modellers at the local lake or pond, the towing of a large model is an experience more for enjoyment and practice than for serious competition. However, serious tug towing in competition with other clubs and with other tug masters or teams is a growing sport. Such competitions, nationally and internationally, are run and governed by rules set by such bodies as the Model Power Boat Association.

Within the membership of the M.P.B.A. are those who have been trained and gained the necessary qualifications to become efficient judges. It is these members who oversee the competition and apply their knowledge to the running of the models over the set courses and to the performances of the tug master or their teams. Generally, the national competitions are organised so that qualifying events are held at various locations throughout the country. Tug masters or teams that win first, and sometimes second and third, places in such area events are then invited to compete at the national finals for the various national trophies. The national tug towing finals are usually held at different clubs waters, ranging between the north and south areas of the country. It is then just possible that a first class team of model tug owners will sometimes be invited to compete abroad.

Currently, the building and sailing of model tugs, whether actually towing or sailing free, is a pleasurable event and enjoyed by many. For some modellers, the actual building of the tug is in itself the ultimate enjoyment. For others, the enjoyment encompasses both building and sailing. There are also those who gain their enjoyment purely by sailing, whilst others are fiercely competitive and who take their delight in competition. Whichever, all can be called tug masters and, it is hoped, all gain equal pleasure in the model tug building and sailing hobby.

Appendices

Appendix 1
Useful Conversion Factors

Length

Inches x 25.4 = millimetres (mm) x 0.0394 = inches
Feet x 0.305 = metres (m) x 3.281 = feet
Miles x 1.609 = kilometres (km) x 0.621 = miles

Volume

Cubic inches x 16.387 = cubic centimetres (cu. Cm) x 0.061 = cubic inches
Imperial Pints x 0.568 = litres (l) x 1.76 = pints
Imperial gallons x 4.456 = litres (l) x 22 = gallons

Weight

Ounces x 28.35 = grams (g) x 0.035 = ounces oz)
Pounds x 0.454 = kilograms (kg) x 2.205 = pounds (lb)

Velocity

Miles per hour (mph) x 1.609 =kilometres/hour (kph) x 0.621 = mph

Temperature

Degrees F = Degrees C x 1.8 + 32 Degrees C = Degrees F – 32 x 0.56

Appendix 2
Suppliers and Publications

Kit Manufacturers

Judoka Ltd, Unit 7,
Model Marin Warehouse,
Hazer, Druidic,
WR9 7DS

Mobile Marine Models,
The Boat Shed,
Highcliffe Park, Ingham Cliff, Lincoln
LN1 2YQ

Deans Marine,
Conquest Drove,
Farcet Fen,
Peterborough
PE7 3DH

The Model Slipway,
Unit 8, Grange Lane Industrial Estate,
Barnsley
S71 5AS

Mount Fleet Models,
Laurel Mount, 7
9, Holmfirth Road,
Meltham,
Huddersfield
HD7 3DA

Nautix – Pocketbond Ltd.,
PO Box 80,
Welwyn
AL6 0ND
Graupner GmbH,
Postfach 1242,

73220 Kichheim/Teck,
Germany

PS Ships,
PO Box 369,
St. Helens,
Merseyside
WA10 9AU

Metcalf Mouldings,
1,Wentworth Cottages,
Haultwick,
Dane End,
Ware
SG11 1JG

Robbe Schluter UK,
Unit 53 Hinckley Workspace,
Southfield Rd,
Hinckley,
LE10 2AS

Specialist Ship Shops

Westbourne Model Centre,
41, Seamoor Road,
Westbourne,
Bournemouth,
BH4 9AE

The Model Dockyard,
17, Tremorvah Barton,
Tregolls Road,
Truro
TR1 1NN

Midway Models,
157, St.Leonards Road,
Leicester
LE2 3BZ

The Dockyard Model Shop,
Ordnance Mews Craft Centre,
The Historic Dockyard,
Chatham
ME4 4TE

Cornwall Model Boats,
Gull Rock,
Treknow,
Tintagel
PL34 0EP

Howes Model Shop,
12, Banbury Road,
Kidlington,
Oxford
OX5 2BT

Scoonie Hobbies,
87, St Clair Street,
Kirkaldy
KY1 2NW

Euromodels,
Woodgreen Farm,
Bulley, Churcham,
Gloucester
GL2 8BJ

Derby Marine Models,
16, George Street,
Derby
DE1 1EH

Suppliers of specialist Equipment

Model Ship Fittings

James Lane Display Models,
30, Broadway,
Blyth
NE24 2PP
    – for etched stanchions etc.

Precision Controls,
3, Chantry Avenue,
Bideford
EX39 2QW

Quay Craft,
Harbour Cottage,
2, Quayfield Road,
Ilfracombe
EX34 9EN

Model Power

Model Propellers etc.

G.T. Sitek,
1, Halton Drive,
Crewe
CW2 8TA

Swan Precision Castings & Engineering Ltd.,
Swan Close Road,
Banbury
OX16 5AL

Electric Motors, etc.

Model Motors Direct,
Keepers Cottage,
Home Farm,
Iwerne Minster
DT11 8LB

Electronic Controls Etc.,

Action-electronics,
19, Carisbrooke Drive,
Nottingham,
NG3 5DS

S.H.G. Model Supplies,
Pinfold Lane,
Wheaton Aston
ST19 9PD

Electronise Design,
2, Hillside Road,
Four Oaks,
Sutton Coldfield
B74 4DQ

Hunter Systems,
24, Aspen Road,
Eastbourne
BN22 0TG

Astec Models & Electronics,
6, Stickland,
Clevedon
BS21 5EX

Steam Outfits

John Hemmens Steam Eng.
28, Breighton Rd.,
Bubwith,
Selby
YO8 6DQ

Stuart Models,
Braye Road,
Vale,
Guernsey
GY3 5XA

Graupner GmbH,
Postfach 1242,
73220 Kichheim/Teck,
Germany

Tony Green Steam Models,
19, Station Road,
Thorpe-on-the-Hill
LN6 9BS

Westbourne Model Centre
– agents for Anton and Heron Steam Outfits
(U.S.A. & France)

Plans Services

Brown Son & Ferguson Ltd.,
4 – 10, Darnley Street,
Glasgow
G41 2SD

David Macgregor Plans,
12, Upper Oldfield Park,
Bath
BA2 3JZ

Jecobin,
31, Romans Way,
Pyrford,
Woking
GU22 8TR

Marine Modelling International,
Traplet Publications Ltd.,
Traplet House,
Severn Drive,
Upton-upon-Severn,
WR8 0JL

Model Boats Plans Service,
MyHobbyStore Ltd,
Berwick House,
8 – 10 Knoll Rise,
Orpington,
BR6 0EL.

Model Shipwright,
Conway Maritime Press,
Anova Books Company Ltd.,
10, Southcombe Street,
London
W14 0RA

Flags & Pennants

B E C C Model Accessories
www.sail-rc.com/

Little Models,
Mike Allsop,
14, The Haverlands,
Goneby Hill Foot,
Grantham
NE31 8HB

Magazines

Marine Modelling International, Traplet Publications
– see above

Model Boats, MyHobbyStore Ltd. – see above

Model Shipwright,
Conway Maritime Press,
Anova Books Company Ltd.,
10, Southcombe Street,
London
W14 0RA

Ships in Focus Record,
J & M Clarkson,
18, Franklands,
Preston
PR4 5PD

Ships Monthly,
222, Branston Road,
Burton-on-Trent,
DE14 3BT

Shipping Today & Yesterday/Sea Breezes,
202 Cotton Exchange Building,
Old Hall Street,
Liverpool
L3 0LA

Appendix 3
Radio Control
Frequencies

27 Megahertz band

Frequency	Flag
26.975	Black
26.995	Brown
27.95	Brown/red
27.45	Red
27.75	Red/orange
27.95	Orange
27.125	Orange/yellow
27.145	Yellow
27.175	Yellow/green
27.195	Green
27.225	Green/blue
27.255	Blue
27.275	Purple

A total of 13 different bands. The split colours are no longer recommended.

40 Megahertz band

Frequency	Flag Number	Frequency	Flag Number
40.665	665	40.835	835
40.675	675	40.845	845
40.685	685	40.855	855
40.695	695	40.865	865
40.705	705	40.875	875
40.715	715	40.885	885
40.725	725	40.895	895
40.735	735	40.905	905
40.745	745	40.915	915
40.755	755	40.925	925
40.765	765	40.935	935
40.775	775	40.945	945
40.785	785	40.955	955
40.795	795	40.965	965
40.805	805	40.975	975
40.815	815	40.985	985
40.825	825	40.995	995

A total of 34 different bands; all to fly a green flag with white numbers thereon.

Appendix 4
Properties of
Saturated Steam

Simplified steam tables

Pressure lbs/sq. inch	Temperature Degrees F	Degrees C*
0.0	212	100
0.0	213	101
1.0	216	102
2.0	219	104
3.0	222	106
4.0	225	107
5.0	228	109
6.0	230	110

Pressure lbs/sq. inch	Temperature Degrees F	Degrees C*
7.0	233	112
8.0	235	113
9.0	237	114
10.0	240	116
11.0	242	117
12.0	244	118
13.0	246	119
14.0	248	120
15.0	250	121
16.0	252	122
17.0	254	123
18.0	255	124
19.0	257	125
20.0	260	127
21.0	261	127
22.0	262	128
23.0	264	129
24.0	265	129
25.0	266	130
26.0	267	131
27.0	270	132
28.0	273	134
29.0	274	134
30.0	276	136
31.0	276	136
33.0	278	137
35.0	281	138
37.0	283	139
39.0	285	140

Pressure lbs/sq. inch	Temperature Degrees F	Degrees C*
41.0	288	142
43.0	290	143
45.0	292	144
47.0	294	146
49.0	296	147
51.0	299	148
53.0	301	149
55.0	302	150
60.0	307	153
65.0	312	156
70.0	316	158
75.0	320	160
85.0	327	164
95.0	334	168
105.0	341	172
115.0	347	175
125.0	353	178

The pressures given above are as read at the boiler pressure gauge at sea level and absolute pressure readings would require the figures above to be increased by 14.696 lbs/sq. inch. The pressures will vary at differing heights above sea level. Temperatures will increase in relation to the degree of heat that is added by drying or superheating the steam after it leaves the boiler.

*Degrees in Centigrade are given as whole numbers, being conversions rounded up or down to the nearest decimal point.

Appendix 5 Navigation Light Details

(All diagrams by kind permission of Bryan Ward)

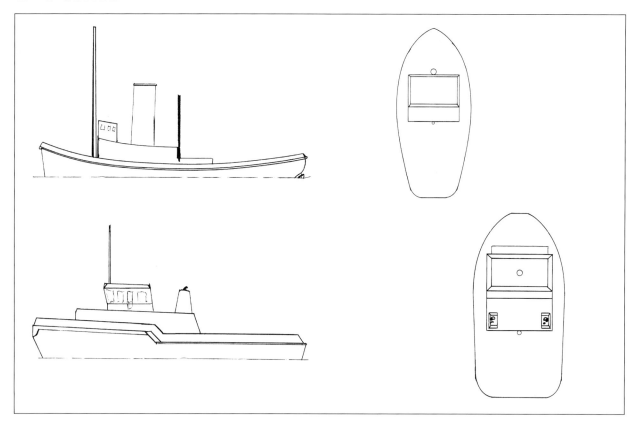

Types of vessel.

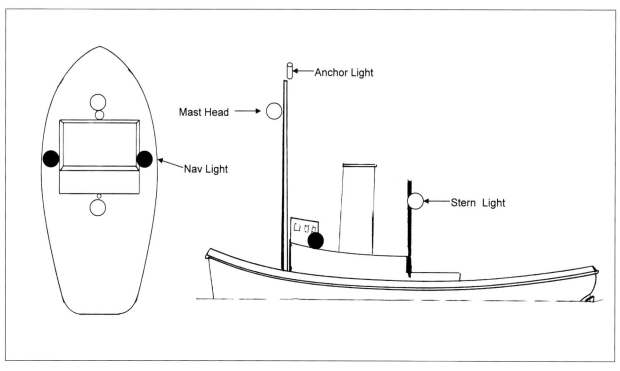

Basic steam boat.

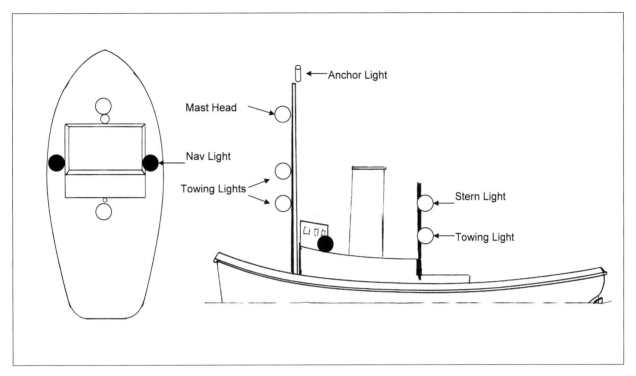

Steam vessel with electric lamps.

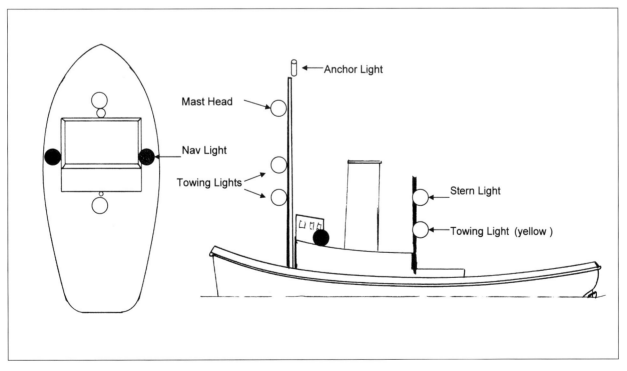

Steam vessel with electric lamps.

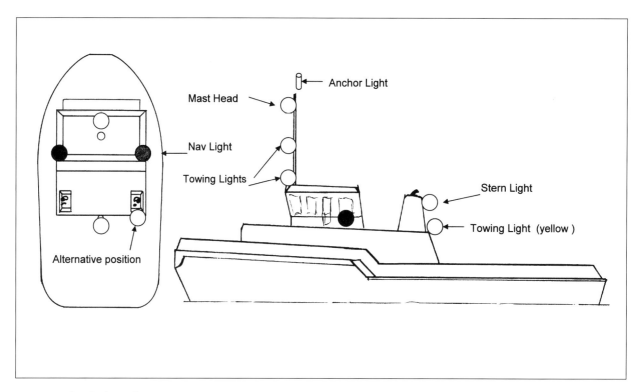

Motor vessel with electric lamps.

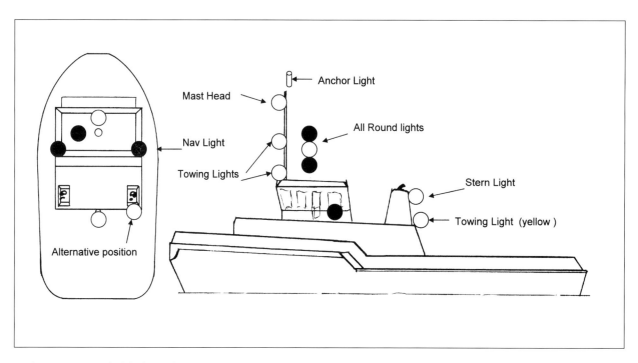

Modern Motor Vessel with electric lamps.

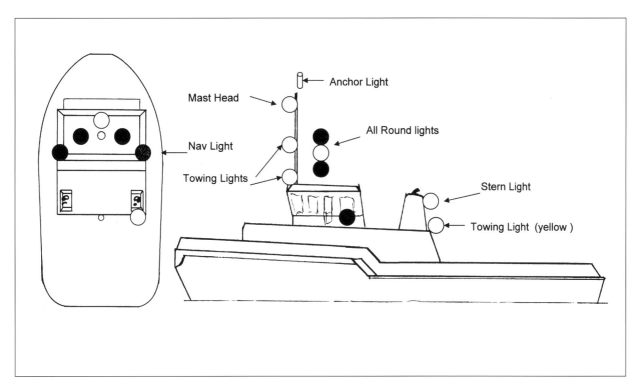

Motor Vessel with electric lamps and alternative positions.

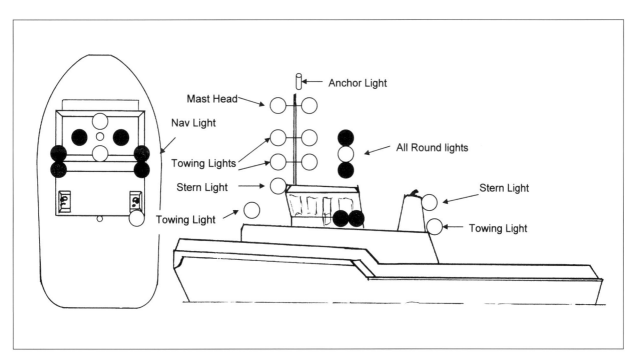

Navigation lamps for a newly registered motor vessel.

Scale Model Tugs